TRAINING THE YOUNG HORSE AND PONY

PRODUCED BY

THE PONY CLUB COUNCIL

1st Edition 1961
2nd Edition 1964
Reprinted 1966
Reprinted 1967
Reprinted 1969
Reprinted 1969
Reprinted 1970
Reprinted 1971

PUBLISHED BY
THE BRITISH HORSE SOCIETY
NATIONAL EQUESTRIAN CENTRE
KENILWORTH, WARWICKSHIRE, CV8 2LR

PRINTED BY
NORTHBOURNE PRESS GROUP LIMITED, COVENTRY

ACKNOWLEDGEMENT

The Pony Club Council gratefully acknowledges the assistance received in the production of this book from Mrs. V. D. S. Williams, Lt.-Col. J. F. S. Bullen, Lt.-Col. A. D. Taylor, Lt.-Col. J. Talbot-Ponsonby, Brig. Keith Dunn and the Editor of 'Riding'.

Illustrations by Joan Wanklyn

CONTENTS

CONTENTS

CONTENTS

ILLUSTRATIONS

ILLUSTRATIONS

ILLUSTRATIONS

FOREWORD

THIS is an official Pony Club publication, recommended as such to all those who are interested in improving their technique in training a horse or pony.

Great care has been taken to select authors who have proved themselves accomplished in their particular field of equitation over many years, but even then each contribution has been carefully reviewed and considered by other acknowledged experts, and when deemed necessary amended with the consent of the author.

Therefore we can say, as we have said of *The Manual of Horsemanship*, the advice to be derived from this publication is advice based upon principles which have stood the test of time to the satisfaction of our most successful horse trainers. Although reference is made to the "pony" throughout the book, the advice given applies equally to horses and to those concerned with their training and improvement.

C. GUY CUBITT

Chairman
The Pony Club

xi

FIGURE I.   WILD MOORLAND PONIES

TRAINING THE YOUNG HORSE AND PONY

INTRODUCTION

One of the reasons for the introduction of the Pony Club Inter-Branch Horse Trials was to improve the standard of training of ponies. There are now a large number of well trained, valuable ponies and many riders who are thoroughly competent to train a young pony.

But there are still far too many badly trained ponies. The reason is nearly always that the early training has been hurried, especially when a young pony shows promise; in consequence he is put to hunting or jumping too soon and what has been omitted can rarely be made good later. If all were trained on sound lines one would less often hear: 'Unfortunately this pony was spoilt before I had him'.

The training syllabus which follows, starts with the newly-born foal in the hope that more ponies will be properly trained from the beginning in the future. Very few riders will be able to start as early as this, but when setting out to train a new pony the rider should ensure, by practical tests, that somebody has carried out this elementary training properly. Is he easy to catch, to handle, to tie up? If not, these things are the first to be taught. How frequently one is told: 'This pony cannot be tied up', or 'This pony cannot be turned out with the others; he will not be caught'.

So let us always make sure that the elementary training has been attended to and the pony taught obedience. Unfortunately

I

one will often find that the pony's training has been neglected, or has been on the wrong lines, and that further training or re-training is necessary. At this stage much harm can be done if short cuts are attempted and quick results looked for. To attempt to force or tie the pony's head in the right position, for example, will not teach him to carry it correctly. This can only be done by following the normal sequence of training, using a snaffle.

For the benefit of riders – and parents – without experience in the training of young ponies, this book has been made as practical and definite as possible.

It is impossible to lay down hard and fast rules as to the age at which the various stages of training are undertaken, as the progress and development differs with every pony. Some develop early, others late; tough, compact ponies are very different from over-grown, perhaps weak ones; thoroughbred two-year-olds which have been well done from birth, are racing at an age when the future hunter may be still out at grass, untouched and perhaps underfed. Every horse and pony, like every human being, is different and it is impossible to generalise or to be dogmatic about them all. The best that one can hope for is that the timetable and programme, outlined in the following pages, may be found suitable for the average pony. In any case it is vitally important to follow the proper sequence of training.

THE TRAINER

To train a pony properly requires knowledge, patience, sympathy, skill, and nerve. You must be quiet, determined and good tempered. Losing control of yourself is a sure step towards losing control of the pony.

You must understand how a pony's mind and body works and

ensure that he is mentally and physically able and has the necessary condition and muscular fitness to carry out what is asked of him. You must be tactful.

You must ride well enough to be able to teach the intended lesson. It is obvious that a rider cannot teach a pony more than he knows himself. For example, if you cannot ride properly over fences on a trained pony, you are not fit to ride a young one over fences – and this applies to any lesson.

Do not attempt to teach more than one new lesson at a time. Reward the pony and end the lesson as soon as he has done what is asked of him.

Ask advice and listen to criticism from those who really understand the subject.

Blame yourself and not the pony if things go wrong.

The average Pony Club rider should be able to train a young pony, or at any rate greatly improve it, by following the principles described in this book. Too much should not be asked of the pony by jumping fences which are too big, or by carrying out movements which are too advanced. Bear in mind that every pony is different both in mind and body and do not expect all to respond in the same way; differences in conformation and condition alone will mean that what comes easily to one may be difficult, tiring or even painful to another.

'There are no bad horses, only bad horsemen'.

THE MIND OF THE HORSE OR PONY

Before attempting to train an animal we must understand how its mind works.

In their wild state, horses and ponies survived because they could go faster than their enemies. Unlike other animals which, when attacked, go to ground, run up a tree or turn and fight, they found safety in flight. To warn them of danger they have very acute senses and very quick reactions; these are particularly active at times of especial danger, as when watering or when suddenly attacked. The water hole, at which all animals congregate, was always a danger to wild horses. So was an enemy, especially one with claws who might spring on their backs; the only hope of survival was to buck him off. Hence, very briefly, we have in the horse or pony an extremely nervous animal whose chance of survival lay in speed or in bucking; one or the other, or both, is the reaction of a frightened or excited pony.

FIGURE 2. ENEMIES

Ponies, like most animals, have good memories of facts; they remember for years places or roads, or other horses; men or things which have frightened them are rarely forgotten.

We teach a horse by associating certain facts in his memory. The fewer the associations connected with the same idea, the stronger they become; for example, jumping may be connected with pleasure and reward, or with pain and fright. This good memory makes mistakes and disobedience dangerous.

Horses have a very limited reasoning power and we have to depend almost entirely on their memories for training. What we do is to command their obedience by forming habits which eventually become so automatic as to be almost second nature, i.e. instinctive.

To understand the mind of the animal to be trained it is essential to be in sympathy with him, to share his feelings and emotions; to anticipate his evasions and to recognise the difference between nervousness, misunderstanding and naughtiness.

Every animal has instincts of self-preservation and self-protection. The young instinctively feed from their mothers. Self-protection is stimulated largely by fear; when frightened, ponies congregate together, run away or buck – all things which we wish to discourage in training.

All ponies are gregarious by nature and like to imitate one another; we can make use of this by giving a pony a lead; on the other hand they will pay attention better if away from others.

A pony enjoys anything which gives him pleasure, e.g. galloping, eating, being caressed or made a fuss of and rewarded.

Finally, when upset he becomes obstinate; every time he gets the better of his rider he becomes worse.

TRAINING

In training, the aim is to produce in the pony a high state of obedience, combined with the full development of his mental and physical powers, for the purpose for which he is intended.

The first thing we have to do is to overcome his fear; this is done by gaining his confidence. We then set out to command obedience and we produce this by forming habits derived from the association of ideas, pleasant or unpleasant, and the use of reward and correction.

For example, the rider teaches the pony to go forward by applying his legs; as soon as the pony moves we relax the pressure. If he does not move we make things unpleasant by the use of a stick. In the end we form a habit. Or again, if he kicks we hit him instantly, so that he may associate the stick with the kick.

A pony must be taught to do what we want and not what he wants; every time he does something that he wants to do and that we do not, he has learnt disobedience; his training has received a set-back and vice versa. Modern training aims at education rather than breaking; it is necessary with ponies to use tact, which might be defined as choosing the right moment to do the right thing. It is unwise to try to teach anything unless everything is in favour of success, for example, do not try to teach a pony to stand still when he is fresh and excited or heading for home, but when he is well exercised, and going away from home.

Always teach anything new when the pony is quiet and obedient, but not tired.

In training we must always consider the effect of condition and temperament; be sure we are not asking too much of the pony. One of the most difficult problems is to decide whether a pony is being naughty, or obstinate, or simply failing to understand our meaning. We can never solve this problem if we lose our tempers.

Young ponies should always be approached quietly and without fear; the trainer's movements should be slow and gentle, never quick or sharp; do not be noisy or frighten a pony. The trainer should be a firm friend – in both senses.

Our system of training therefore is reward and correction. Reward, when the pony does well, is given by stopping the lesson, patting him and giving him freedom of his head and a long rein; or by giving him a carrot or handful of oats; or by dismounting and taking him home, but always by giving instant relief, so that this is associated with his obedience and a successful lesson. Correction takes the form of repeating or intensifying the lesson or, in the last resort, of punishment.

Never punish when you are angry (do not set your teeth!) and make sure that the pony knows what he is being punished for.

Both reward and correction should be immediate.

Summary

A pony has strong instincts – fear being one of the strongest. He has little reasoning power but a very good memory.

We therefore develop the habit of obedience by the association of ideas; these associations must be perfectly clear and we must be quite certain that the pony knows what we want. We aim at making the habit so automatic that eventually it becomes second nature, i.e. practically instinctive.

Reward and correction is our guiding principle.

Blame yourself and not the pony.

FEEDING AND CONDITION

This subject is admirably dealt with in *The Manual of Horsemanship* under 'Health, condition and exercise' and will not be repeated here.

But it is important (a) to give a pony sufficient food and exercise for his physical development: (b) to avoid excessive feeding which will cause a pony to get over-excited, above himself, or too fat and heavy; (c) to avoid too much work which may over-strain a pony and cause lameness, muscle fatigue, breakdowns or obstinacy and 'nappiness'.

Feeding, exercise and training must therefore be correctly balanced to obtain the best results.

STAGE I

Preliminary training and breaking

The first object in training a pony is to give him confidence and make him realise that man is his friend. At the same time he must learn obedience and respect for his trainer. He must move willingly and freely and his muscles must remain supple. He must grow in mind and body and increase in strength and obedience.

The foal

The earlier the handling of the foal commences the better; within a few days of foaling, a slip can be put on for a few minutes each day and the foal held by it and then led about. The sooner the feet are picked up the quicker will the habit be confirmed and the foal will not be strong enough to resist much. As time goes on the feet may be touched up with the rasp and the first lesson in shoeing will be learnt. Brushing the mud off the coat will soon get the foal used to the idea of grooming. When leading starts it is better to have two people, one of whom leads the mare and the other the foal; the foal should be led close to the mare and gradually be made to walk further away during the next two or three months. From the very start he must be led with both the right and the left hand of the trainer and in large circles to right and left; turns, too, must be to either hand, the proper turn being to the side away from the trainer. This is an important point, for a foal which is always led and turned to the same side is well on the way to developing a stiff side, a one-sided mouth and a dislike for turning one way.

If the dam comes when called and is easy to catch, the foal will soon do the same; if he has not learnt with his mother this must be one of the first lessons after he has been weaned. He must always be rewarded when he comes; he will get confidence in his trainer and associate coming when called with a suitable reward. Throughout his training, obedience and discipline must be insisted upon and enforced by reward or correction. It will be noted that the dam enforces quite considerable discipline herself, laying back her ears, baring her teeth and 'scolding' the foal with angry faces if he does wrong.

FIGURE 3.   THE FIRST LESSON—COMING WHEN CALLED

Quite early in life the foal may have to be boxed with the mare – perhaps when eight or nine days old, when the mare visits the stallion. Or the pair of them may go to a show. Showing is admirable for the foal, which learns to travel, to be led and shown in hand, to leave the dam and to become accustomed to all the strange sights and sounds of the showground. Whether at a show or at home the foal has to become quiet with motors, tractors, traffic and other animals. This early training is valuable.

Little training will be done during the first winter, in the early part of which the foal will be weaned. Handling for feeding, trimming the feet and shutting up at night will continue; he may be tied up for short periods and a rug and surcingle put on him so that he may not be frightened by it. If feeding involves going through a gateway, a small log may be placed across it and so the first lesson in crossing an obstacle is learnt.

The yearling

When training recommences in the spring, the previous summer's lessons should be repeated and confirmed. The yearling will now be led about the farm, on roads and in the village, alone. He should become accustomed to all forms of traffic, to being 'boxed', and to other animals, including dogs and farm animals. If he is shown, he will be made to walk round quietly, to walk and trot up and to stand properly – the last a very valuable lesson for later in life. If he is not shown he must be taught these things at home and also become accustomed to being groomed, trimmed and having his feet attended to.

The importance of leading and turning to either right or left hand must always be kept in mind.

With young animals, lessons should be kept short; three lessons of ten minutes each are of far greater value than one lesson of thirty minutes.

During these early lessons the pony should be taught to obey the trainer's voice both inside and outside the stable. Not only will he come when called, 'get over' in the stable and 'hold up' his foot, but he will walk on and stop when told to, when being led in hand.

The two-year-old

After a second winter similar to the first, training will start again in the spring, the pony now being two years old.

All the work done during the previous summer should be repeated and confirmed before any new lessons are undertaken.

Lungeing

If the pony is fit and strong, lungeing may be done for a short time every day, but if he is weak or backward this should not be started yet.

For lungeing it is important to use the proper tack and to have it correctly fitted. A cavesson is much to be preferred to an ordinary head collar; the latter easily gets pulled out of position, while a cavesson, heavier and more rigid, remains steady and gives much more control. It should be carefully fitted, especially the nose-band and throatlash. The latter should be fairly tight so that the side pieces cannot come forward and injure the pony's eye. A long webbing lungeing rein is attached to the centre ring on the nose-band. It should never be attached to the bit, when fitted, as this will injure the pony's mouth. To start with, a bit should not be fitted and there is no hurry to do so. Later on, when the pony is going well on the lunge a snaffle or key bit may be fitted. It is important that the pony should be used to the bit and going kindly with it, before the time comes for mounting for the first time.

A body roller, to which side-reins of similar length are attached from each side to the nose-band, is also used; it has the further use of preparing the young animal for the girth. It is better not to fit the body roller until the pony is going kindly on the lunge. When it is fitted for the first time the pony may well 'play up', so this should be done in a loose-box or school. It should be tightened gently. The side-reins should not be tight but sufficiently **short** to prevent the pony carrying his head to one side or too high. It is an advantage to put boots on all four legs to save the pony from hitting himself or brushing. If much work is to be done on hard ground the pony should have shoes on. A long whip is required to keep the pony moving forward and away from the trainer; it should however be shown to the pony and not used for hitting him. This completes the equipment required for lungeing.

FIGURE 4. PREPARATION FOR LUNGEING

The object of lungeing is to teach the young pony obedience; to assist him to develop his muscles, action and balance; to teach him lessons, especially at the trot, which could otherwise only be done mounted, and to prepare him for subsequent stages when ridden.

To begin with, an assistant is required. To circle the pony to the left, the trainer gathers the rein in loops in his left hand, starting with the loop at the end of the lunge rein, and holds the whip in his right hand. With the rein held four or five yards long he will tell his assistant to hold the pony by the cavesson on the same (near) side and to walk round him in a small circle. The pony and the assistant should start when the trainer says 'walk on' or clicks his tongue, at the same time showing his whip. This should not be used in such a way as to frighten the pony but just to make him walk on. Quickly he will learn to associate the word and the whip with moving on. The trainer should make the pony walk in front of him all the time so that he can see the buttock farthest from him and has the feeling that he is driving the pony before him. He should not walk after the pony nor step backwards to keep the rein tight but keep stepping round on the same spot. When the pony is going quietly he should be stopped by word of command, with the help of the assistant. After doing this a few times the trainer should stop; he and the assistant should go to the other side of the pony, change the rein and whip into the other hands and repeat the performance, going the opposite way round. This will be enough for one day – not more than twenty minutes.

FIGURE 5.   LUNGEING WITH THE HELP OF AN ASSISTANT

When the lesson is finished the trainer should not walk towards the pony but insist on the pony coming up to him. The trainer should step slowly back as the pony comes towards him; a youngster, or a pony of any age for that matter, will always come to you if you step back, not forward.

Control is easier if lungeing is done in the corner of a field, with some poles lying across the open sides.

After a few days it may be possible to dispense with the assistant, but if there is any trouble call him back rather than have a scene or frighten the pony with the whip. After a few weeks – there is really no hurry as the rate of progress must depend upon the development of the pony – he may be trotted but cantering should not be attempted until he is much older, stronger, and better balanced. Special attention should be paid to making the pony move around the circle with long, regular strides and an even rhythm.

When it is decided to allow him to canter, he must be encouraged, by voice and whip, to strike off calmly and gently on the correct inner leg. If he starts on the wrong leg he must be checked at once, brought back to a trot, and started off again. Care must be taken

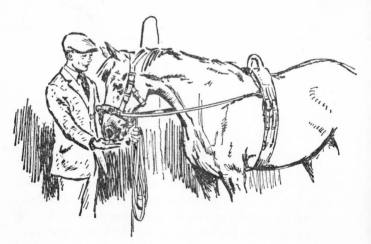

FIGURE 6.   ALWAYS REWARD THE PONY WHEN HE DOES RIGHT

that the hind feet follow in the tracks of the fore feet; if there is too strong a pull on the rein, the pony's head will be turned inwards and the quarters and hind legs will fly out. This can be prevented to some extent by using the corner of a field or manege.

All this time there must be insistence on obedience to the voice and whip; the pony must be made to halt and stand still and square, with his weight on all four feet; this is not easy. Lungeing for ten minutes or so, preferably twice a day, is sufficient to begin with. This should be varied with other work already carried out. Work at the increase and decrease of pace – walk, trot, walk, halt, stand, etc., but not always in the same sequence.

Always reward the pony when he does right.

Backing and mounting for the first time

Racehorses, which are very well done from birth, are backed during their second winter and raced as two-year-olds. With hunters, which may not be so well done (fed) and mature more slowly, serious work does not begin until two or three years later than this, although their preliminary training may start earlier. Ponies probably come somewhere between the two, but it is important to realise that if young animals are worked too strenuously they will suffer for it later.

Towards the end of the summer, perhaps during the holidays, a two-year-old pony may be backed. The more he has been handled and the earlier in life he is backed, the simpler this is likely to be. In fact if an animal has been properly prepared, it is very rare to have any trouble at all. If backing is deferred until the pony is four years old or more, he will be much stronger, more independent and more likely to be difficult; on the other hand if the pony is ridden when too young or by too heavy a person, damage may easily be caused.

Before attempting to mount, the pony should have been worked regularly for some weeks, be going quietly and obediently and be able to carry out the lessons so far described, both on and off the lungeing rein. He should have been carrying a saddle instead of a body roller. This preparatory work is very important. At the end of a steady week's work and when daily exercise has been completed, arrangements for mounting may be made. The ideal place is a riding school but a loose-box is suitable, or even the corner of a quiet paddock.

Leading the pony up to the mounting block and making much of him has already been included in the daily training. So that by this time the pony is quite used to seeing the trainer above him on the mounting block – on both sides of course.

If he is to be mounted in the open the pony may be stood beside a mounting block or a large box, saddled, with stirrups down, and a stirrup leather round his neck for use as a 'holding-on' strap.

FIGURE 7 (a). BACKING—A LEG-UP

FIGURE 7 (*b*). BACKING—SECOND STAGE—LEANING ACROSS THE SADDLE

An assistant should hold the pony. The trainer, with his feet on
the mounting block, should then lean across the saddle a few times,
gradually increasing the weight, patting and speaking to the pony
at the same time. If the pony is backed inside the stable, it is
better to dispense with a mounting block and if possible to have
another assistant to give a quiet leg-up.

After a few days, depending on the progress, when the pony is
accustomed to taking the weight calmly, the trainer may carry his
right leg across, being careful not to touch the quarters, and sit in
the saddle, taking the stirrups and holding the neck strap with one
hand and the reins with the other. The assistant is responsible for
the pony, the trainer for remaining 'on top'. It is very rare for a

FIGURE 7 (c). BACKING—THIRD STAGE—SETTLED QUIETLY IN THE SADDLE

pony to 'put up a show' but if he does it is important to stay put and let the pony know that he cannot dislodge his rider. Next, the pony should be moved forward a step or two and turned – this is the moment when he is most likely to buck and the rider must refrain from using his legs. Provided all is going well, it is now a matter of gradually increasing the time spent in the saddle ; but with a two-year-old pony this should not exceed twenty minutes at the most. The rider should mount and dismount from both sides. The assistant can be dispensed with when the pony has settled down and is going quietly.

The pony should be ridden in a snaffle bridle or with the reins on the cavesson nose-band.

This concludes his two-year-old training; he should be allowed to grow and develop during the winter. To 'keep his hand in' he can be ridden about for a short time at a walk when opportunity offers, but he must not be given any strenuous exercise. He should now be ready to begin his serious mounted training in the spring.

During all this time, especially during the winter, the pony must receive suitable but not excessive feeding.

'Make haste slowly'.

STAGE II

Elementary training

The objects to be attained at this stage are confidence, obedience and suppleness. The pony must learn to go freely forward on the bit and to be responsive to the rider's leg aids.

Provided he is strong and has developed well, this stage may begin when the pony is three years old. Even then he should not be ridden for longer than half-an-hour at a time.

All previous training must be repeated and confirmed, especially lungeing which can be carried out by a trainer too heavy to ride the pony. If the pony has not been ridden for some time, the preliminary work carried out before he was mounted for the first time must be repeated before mounting again. A set-back must be avoided.

Correct bitting

Correct bitting is very important. At this stage all the work should be done in a snaffle ; a thick, jointed snaffle is the best type and a good pattern is illustrated. It has cheek pieces which prevent the bit from rubbing the sides of the pony's mouth, or from being pulled through the mouth to one side or the other. Note the small 'keeper' fastening the cheek piece of the bit to the cheek piece of the bridle ; this prevents the bit from turning over in the

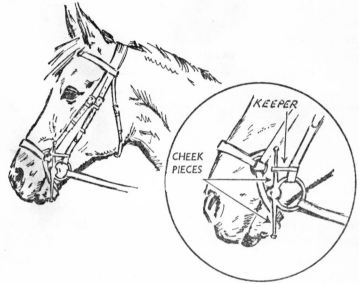

FIGURE 8.   SNAFFLE BRIDLE AND DROPPED NOSEBAND

mouth so that it is always in the same position.   If a young pony
gets hold of the end of the cheek piece in his mouth, a simple ring
or egg-butt snaffle may be used.

Another type which is used for young ponies is the straight bar
snaffle, with either a plain steel or wooden mouthpiece, with or
without keys.   There is no pinching action with the bar snaffle.
The keys encourage the pony to play with the bit and this keeps
his mouth wet and soft.   This is a good bit for mouthing the
pony in the stable, but not good to use when riding him.

The headstall should be adjusted so that the snaffle touches the
corners of the mouth without pulling them up. If it is too high it
will rub the corners of the mouth; if too low it will encourage the
pony to play with it with his tongue and learn bad habits, such as

putting the tongue over the bit. It is advisable to fit a nose-band with a snaffle; a dropped nose-band, fitted below the bit, is effective in preventing a pony from opening his mouth, but it must not be too tight and the upper strap must be fitted sufficiently high not to interfere with the nostrils and breathing.

From the start, the pony must be taught to stand still for mounting and dismounting from either side and also to stand squarely on all four feet, both with and without the rider.

Free forward movement

As soon as he has been mounted, the pony must learn to move freely forward in response to the rider's leg aids assisted, at first, by the voice and whip. He must recover his natural balance under the weight of his rider, his head and neck being allowed to find their own position. He must go straight, with reins held long, and no effort must be made to collect him. At the walk he should be ridden without contact until he has learnt to accept the bit at the trot; this he will do only gradually, as he becomes more responsive to the rider's legs. He must be made to move freely and actively, taking long, level strides. There will be frequent halts, with very little contact. The pace will be increased and decreased – halt to walk, walk to trot, trot to walk, walk to halt; but not always in the same order and done very gradually.

When he will move freely in a straight line, large circles may be made at the walk and trot using an 'open' rein, with the pony's head bent slightly in the direction in which he is going and with the hind feet following in the track of the fore feet. (See Fig. 9).

The application of the aids on a young pony must be clear, definite and even exaggerated. Allow time for the pony to understand and interpret an aid before applying it again. Some ponies are quick to understand whereas others are slow and get very easily muddled. As the training proceeds the aids will become more

FIGURE 9.   FIRST LESSON IN CIRCLING—OPEN REIN

delicate until, with the trained pony, they become practically
invisible to the onlooker whilst at the same time maintaining their
clarity to the pony.

Every aid requires the complete harmony of body, legs and
hands, without which it is quite impossible to get smooth results,

and the aids must be sustained to the necessary degree throughout all movements. By placing the pony in the correct position before the aid is given, the pony can obey more easily what the aid indicates. Place before you propel.

It is important for the rider when riding at the trot to change the diagonal frequently and always when making a change of direction. If a pony is always ridden on the same diagonal he will go unevenly and become stiff on one side owing to the unequal development of his muscles. It is suggested that the rider 'sits' on the left diagonal (near-fore and off-hind) when on the right rein and vice versa, which has the tendency to bring the inside

FIGURE 10.   LEAVING HIS FIELD AND HIS COMPANIONS

hind leg more under the body thus making it easier to get round curves.

No effort should be made to pull the pony's head into position or to tie it there. The back muscles which carry the weight of the rider will become fatigued so the pony should not be worked for more than a few minutes at a time. At the end of every lesson there should be a period at the walk with the reins held long before dismounting and rewarding the pony. Rest is the greatest reward; therefore there must be a rest at the end of a lesson and when a movement has been correctly performed. When a pony responds and does something correctly, the trainer should stop; he should not repeat over and over again until the pony, from boredom or fatigue or sourness, does it wrong. Young ponies easily get soured.

The pony should go happily and freely away from his field or stable, and from other ponies, especially his own companions. (See Fig. 10).

Loose jumping

At this stage, jumping lessons over very small obstacles may begin. If the pony has been used to walking over a pole in a gateway from early days he will take kindly to being led over poles, small tree trunks and little ditches. He may be sent round a jumping lane or loose school, if available, with the fences on the ground and later raised to a foot or so high.

An oval lane is better than a straight one; ponies are less likely to rush and the trainer, single-handed, can walk round in the centre and keep the pony going. If the lane is too big, the trainer has difficulty in keeping up; if too small, the pony does not get a straight run at the fences and has too little room to correct his stride. Suitable outside measurements are 25 yards by 15 yards, with the track and fences 9 feet wide. See Figure 11 (a).

The fences, which should be solid, must be varied and should include a ditch, parallel poles to give width and, as training pro-

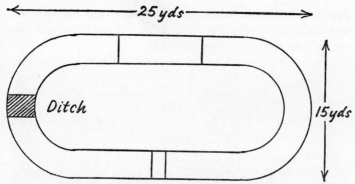

FIGURE 11 (a).   DIAGRAM OF OVAL JUMPING LANE

gresses, a double. It must be easy for a trainer, who is not very
strong, to alter the height of the fences; a simple method of doing
so is shown in Figure 11 (b); it consists of two upright posts, with

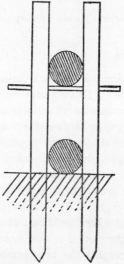

FIGURE 11 (b).   DIAGRAM—CROSS-SECTION OF ADJUSTABLE JUMP SUPPORT

holes bored every six inches, through which an iron pin is pushed; on this pin rests a pole. For a higher fence two or even three poles can be fixed between two pair of posts.

FIGURE 12.   OVAL JUMPING LANE—TRAINER IN CORRECT POSITION

Lungeing over fences

If the trainer is sufficiently expert with the lungeing rein, the pony may be lunged over fences. This is a very useful method of schooling, for it enables a person who is too heavy to ride to teach a pony to jump and may be continued throughout his life, when further schooling to correct faults or restore confidence is necessary. The usual tack for lungeing, already described, should be used, but without side-reins, which might prevent him from lowering his head and making use of his neck. One or more fences, similar to those in the oval lane, are required. The fence should have one end by a hedge or wall and at the other should be a wing consisting of a long pole with the end on the ground so that there is nothing in which the rein might get caught; the arrangement is shown in the diagram.

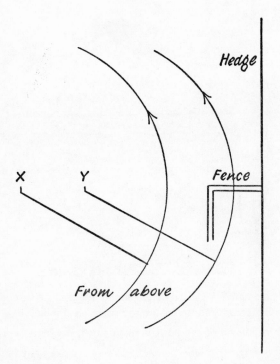

FIGURE 13. DIAGRAM—LUNGEING OVER A FENCE—THE TRAINER'S POSITION

The trainer stands, as in the diagram, at x and circles the pony in the usual way on the lungeing rein, first left and then right. At this stage there should be no pole in position, only the uprights and the wing. When the pony is going freely the trainer gradually moves forward to y, allowing the pony to make a slightly larger circle which will bring him beyond the wing and between the uprights. After he has made half a dozen circles correctly the pole may be inserted on the ground between the uprights; this will gradually be raised as progress is made. Later on fences will be

FIGURE 14. LUNGEING OVER A FENCE

varied; a small 'spread' fence of parallel poles must be one of the first to be introduced, to ensure the correct parabola.

The impulsion of the pony is maintained, i.e. he is kept going, by the use of the whip.

This would normally complete the training to be expected of an average pony at the age of three, but with a backward one some of it might be deferred until the following year.

Further elementary training

As the pony's strength and training develops, further progress may be demanded of him. This stage may start at four years old and continue throughout the next year or two.

The objects now will be to make him more supple and obedient, to improve his balance and to teach him to respond to simple aids. He should accept light contact with the bit and go straight and freely forwards with an even cadence. He should jump small, varied fences calmly and alone and be a good hack, with manners.

He can be taken out hunting for short days.

All the previous training should be continued, with a higher standard of obedience and better performance. The pony should go forward to the lightest pressure of the rider's legs.

He may now be expected to accept a light contact with the bit. This should be taught at the trot, on a long rein, encouraging him

FIGURE 15. ACCEPTING A LIGHT CONTACT WITH THE BIT

to feel for the bit and extend his head and neck forwards and downwards. He should go freely, lengthening but not quickening his stride, with an even cadence.

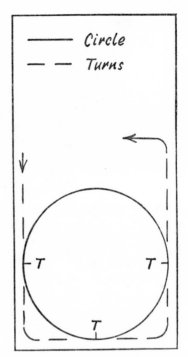

FIGURE 16 (a).   DIAGRAM—CIRCLES AND TURNS

Circles, turns and loops

Work should now be done on circles, which may gradually be reduced in size, but never to a diameter of less than twenty yards. These circles must be correctly executed, with the pony bent slightly inwards and the hind feet following in the track of the fore feet. As the pony improves, the rein will not need to be so 'open' ; it will gradually become more direct. One must always remember, when feeling the inner rein in a turn, to allow the outer hand to go slightly forward so as not to pull in the head and check the forward movement but not so as to allow too much bend, particularly to the side the pony likes turning best.

When circles are done correctly, turns may be made. At first these should not be too sharp. Loops are another excellent exercise, the rider insisting on a correct bend with each change of rein.

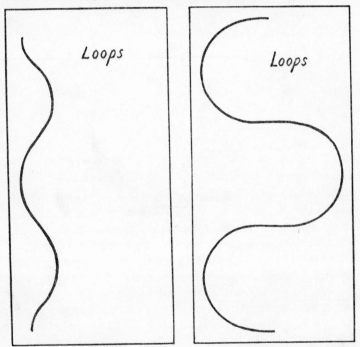

FIGURE 16 (b).   DIAGRAM LOOPS (SERPENTINE)

The diagrams above show a circle, turns and loops. When making a circle in a manege it is important to touch the track round the school at *T* and to make a true circle, not a series of turns.

FIGURE 17. CIRCLE AND CHANGE OF REIN

The canter

Work at the canter will start early in this stage, but not until the pony is obedient at the trot and responds to the rider's aids. It is better to teach him to strike off with the correct leg from the start. The first cantering lesson should be on a big circle in the corner of a field or in the manege (see Fig. 16(a)), with the pony trotting steadily. When he gets near the corner on the left rein, for example, the rider's right leg should be drawn back behind the girth, the pony's head bent slightly to the left and with a strong pressure of the rider's legs, seat and back, the pony will be made to strike off into a canter. If he strikes off on the wrong leg, he should be brought quietly back to a trot and the lesson repeated. Success is largely a matter of the rider's rhythm and timing of the aids. It is a mistake to rush along at a fast trot, urging the pony to canter; in this way it becomes a matter of chance on which leg the pony strikes off and there is a lack of balance and control. If the pony has been correctly trained on the lunge, there will be no difficulty in teaching him to canter. The voice can be used at first and then dropped when the pony understands the aids.

FIGURE 18. TEACHING A PONY TO CANTER

Although it is better to teach the young pony to strike off on the correct leg from the start, it may sometimes be advisable, with a lazy pony and perhaps a not very strong rider, to concentrate on a quiet transition from the trot to the canter, irrespective of which

FIGURE 18. TEACHING A PONY TO CANTER

FIGURE 19. REDUCING PACE—CANTER TO TROT

leg he leads with. As the pony becomes more responsive and training progresses he may be taught to lead with the correct leg.

To come back to a trot from the canter, keep the pony's hocks under him by using the seat and leg aids; resist with the hands and quietly 'ask' with the rein on the side on which the pony resists and let him drop gently back into a trot. It is important that he does not throw up his head, therefore the rider must be gentle with his hands. To begin with, when slowing down, the pony may be allowed to have his balance rather more forward than

FIGURE 19. REDUCING PACE—CANTER TO TROT

would be the case with a trained pony, but as he gains in strength his hocks will gradually be brought more underneath him.

Canter equally on either leg. It is a good plan, when hacking and when riding from covert to covert, to canter with a different leading leg in alternate fields. Long steady cantering in straight lines is calming and helps to improve the action.

Turn on the forehand

This movement teaches the pony to move away from the leg.

FIGURE 20.   MOVING THE QUARTERS—A NECESSARY MOVEMENT

It is very useful when opening a gate mounted, as it enables the rider to place his pony in the correct position. It is also helpful out hunting to turn a pony's heels quickly away from hounds in a road.

The pony must be standing squarely on all four legs and be holding the bit lightly in his mouth. It is most important not to attempt to start this exercise if there is any resistance whatsoever in the pony's mouth. To turn to the right on the forehand, the rider gently 'asks' with the right rein, but should not turn the pony's head more than just enough to make his right eye visible. With

Pivot

Fence or Wall

FIGURE 21. TURN ON THE FOREHAND

the right leg drawn back behind the girth he pushes the pony's quarters over to the left. The rider's left leg remains at the girth to keep him from stepping backwards and to help send him forward the moment the turn is completed (see Fig. 17). It is not a good thing to halt after a turn on the forehand because the pony is apt to lose forward impulsion, and he can easily put up an evasion by getting behind the bit.

In the turn to the right, the off-fore is the pivoting leg, which can either actually pivot, or be picked up and put down again in the same place. The pony's off-hind leg should cross over in front of the near-hind. He must on no account step backwards. To start with, only two steps should be asked for and the pony sent forward again; gradually ask for more and more until a full half-turn can be made without any resistance from the pony and with a perfectly still head-carriage. To turn to the left on the forehand, reverse the aids.

Simple change of leg (canter – trot – canter)

When the pony has a correct head-carriage, can 'carry himself', and is obedient to the aids for a canter, he may be taught the simple change of leg, through the trot. This should not be expected until towards the end of this stage. The pony is brought back from the canter to a trot and, after a few strides, is made to strike off again on the opposite leg. This is most easily done first on a large figure of eight, using the whole school, if in a manege; later it can be done on a loop and finally on a straight line.

Technically, as a dressage movement, the simple change of leg consists of coming from a canter to a walk and back to a canter on the opposite leg. This movement would be too advanced at the present stage ; at first it should be done progressively through a trot.

By now the pony should be capable of doing the Pony Club Dressage Test.

Other exercises

Circles can be reduced to a diameter of ten yards at a trot and twenty at a canter. This must be done gradually; if the pony loses impulsion, balance or cadence, it is an indication that the circle is too small and should be enlarged.

To improve his balance, the pony can be ridden up and down hill at all paces and over ridge and furrow; quite steep hills are to be encouraged, but they must be taken slowly, with the pony under control, and care taken that he is kept straight. These exercises teach him to look where he is putting his feet. He should also walk through fords and thick, 'blind' places, and stand while gates are opened with hand and whip.

FIGURE 22.   IMPROVING BALANCE
GOOD MANNERS MUST BE INSISTED UPON

There must be work on a loose rein; not only will this help the pony to find his balance and 'carry himself' but it will make him a pleasanter ride and a better hack.

Work in the open is important at this stage; there is more natural impulsion than when riding in an enclosed manege or in the corner of a field and the pony will go with more freedom.

Good manners must be insisted upon. He must stand still when required; he must be quiet when alone and with other ponies, in traffic, with machines, dogs and farm animals (how many ponies dislike pigs!) and with a whip and polo stick.

Manners, good or bad, are catching. If yours are uncouth and rough your pony's may be the same.

'Manners maketh horse and rider'.

Stable manners are equally important and are very largely a matter of early handling; the pony must allow his feet to be picked up and his ears pulled, be quiet to shoe, clip, trim and groom; he should go kindly into a trailer or box.

Jumping when mounted

Before attempting mounted schooling on a young pony it is absolutely essential that the trainer should be able to ride over a fence well enough, not only not to interfere with the pony's action, but to maintain a correct position in which to control the pony. This is described in *The Manual of Horsemanship* under 'Jumping'.

When a pony will lead or lunge kindly over small obstacles, or go quietly round a jumping lane, and will go forward freely in response to the rider's leg aids, he may be ridden over small and simple fences. Already accustomed to jumping loose and being led over fences, he now has to adapt himself to carrying the rider's weight.

Before discussing mounted schooling, it is necessary to study the pony in the approach, the take-off, the period of suspension and the landing.

During the approach the pony lowers his head and neck, and stretches the neck. This enables him to balance himself and prepare to make his jump.

As he takes off the pony shortens his neck slightly, raises his head, and lifts his forehand off the ground. He brings his hocks under him, stretches his head and neck and makes his spring upward and forward.

During the period of suspension the head and neck are stretched to the full extent forwards and downwards. The hind legs, having left the ground, are gathered up under the belly.

As the pony lands his head comes up and his neck shortens.

This can be well understood by watching the Pony Club film 'Jumping', or any good film of horses jumping.

All ponies, and especially young ones, should enjoy jumping; the rider must do nothing to spoil this enjoyment. He must not interfere with the mouth nor have his weight on the loins during the jump; it is useful to have a neck strap to hold on to, in case of an awkward jump; the mane can serve the same purpose.

A start should be made by walking over a heavy pole or log on the ground, varied with other logs and small ditches. After a week

FIGURE 23.   JUMPING WHEN MOUNTED

or two increase the height, e.g. a tree trunk, and width (two parallel logs and wider ditches). When enlarging jumps it is better to widen them rather than always to raise them. In order to cover the extra width the pony will have to jump higher.

The trot is the best pace at this stage; it is less effort than jumping from a walk and easier than when cantering, for the pony to balance himself and to judge the take-off.

As he progresses, the width and height may be increased, but for the first year or so they must be kept very small – for a 14·2 h.h. pony probably not more than two feet. If he is overfaced he will soon learn to refuse instead of developing the habit of jumping whatever his trainer puts him at. Instead of increasing the size, introduce variety – banks, little walls, coloured poles, wet, dry and 'blind' ditches, easy doubles, cavalletti, fences up and down hill and drops. Schooling fences should be solid; if they are not the pony will knock them down instead of learning to adjust his stride when meeting a fence 'wrong' and out of stride. There should be as many spread fences – ditches, parallel poles or tree trunks – as upright.

For notes on the construction of fences see the chapter on 'Jumping' in *The Manual of Horsemanship*.

3   4

There is no hurry to start cantering; it is a great asset to have a pony which will jump a good spread from a trot. It is an easy matter to make a pony jump quickly but more difficult to stop him 'rushing'. When the trainer does start jumping at a canter, he must ride hard enough to make the pony take-off well away and jump properly.

See that the pony jumps in good style, looking at the fence, using his head and neck and 'tipping' well. His stride must be calm and cadenced before and after the jump and the rider must ensure that he suffers no pain in mouth, loins or legs. It is most important that the pony is on the bit and keeps his head still during the approach; this will largely depend upon the rider keeping his hands still and gentle. He must jump with a good parabola, neither too flat nor too much 'up and down'. There must be no excitement but plenty of enjoyment.

The pony may now be taken out hunting for an hour or two and commence elementary hunter trials and show jumping, provided he is jumping well, keenly and in good style.

Correcting jumping faults

Due to a variety of reasons, enumerated below, jumping training sometimes does not go according to plan and faults appear.

A pony is considered to jump well when he approaches the fence with confidence and at an even pace, as directed by the rider, takes off at such a distance from the fence as to make the least possible effort necessary to clear the jump, jumps with a supple neck and back and lands quietly to continue at the desired pace.

A pony jumps badly when he approaches the fence nervously, refuses, runs out, or props at the take-off and bucks over, or rushes into the fence with his head in the air and is over excited.

Common causes of bad jumping and refusals

(1) Lack of training.

(2) The pony being asked to jump fences that are too big or difficult for the stage of training.

(3) Falls and subsequent lack of nerve.

(4) Weakness and lack of condition.

(5) The pony being sore from splint, tendon, foot, etc.

(6) Badly fitted and uncomfortable saddle or bridle.

(7) Memories of pain caused by a job in the mouth, etc.

(8) The rider over-shortening the stride during the approach.

(9) Bad presentation of the pony to the fence and lack of determination by the rider.

FIGURE 24. A JOB IN THE MOUTH WILL NOT BE FORGOTTEN

The cure for any of the above is first to diagnose the cause correctly, and then to use common sense to counteract it.

(7), (8) and (9) are clear indications that the rider is not good enough to school a young pony. The training must either be undertaken by somebody else, or the rider must set out to improve his riding under the supervision of an instructor. When he starts schooling again, he should follow the procedure outlined for (2) below, for a pony which has been overfaced.

(4), (5) and (6) are matters of stable management.

In the case of (4), weakness and lack of condition, it would be well to take the advice of the veterinary surgeon or an experienced stud groom. Probably the first points needing attention will be to

FIGURE 25.　AN UNCOMFORTABLE BRIDLE WILL CAUSE BAD JUMPING

file the teeth, and to dose for worms. Then follow the advice given in *The Manual of Horsemanship* under 'Health, condition and exercise'.

For (5), lameness, get the blacksmith to examine the foot and call in the vet.

If the fault lies in a badly fitting saddle or bridle (6), it should obviously be correctly fitted and adjusted if possible. But it may be that the bridle or bit is too large or too small, and that even by punching more holes it still cannot be made to fit. The only answer here is to beg, borrow or buy another.

Many saddles are in poor condition. Make sure that the saddle is correctly stuffed, fits the young pony, and does not pinch the withers or press upon the spine. Do not ride if the pony is galled.

(1), (2) and (3) indicate that training has been inadequate or wrongly carried out. This will often prove to be the case when a new pony is purchased.

Make a start with (1) and follow the instructions for 'Loose jumping' at the beginning of Stage II. If all goes well assume that

FIGURE 26.   FENCES WHICH ARE TOO BIG

the pony has been overfaced as in (2) or frightened as in (3) by falls or by hurting himself. Often it is the rider who is feeling nervous! Therefore lower the fences, laying poles on the ground at first, and get the pony going freely, only raising the fences again very gradually. When schooling, it is always advisable to keep the fences small so that the pony will jump anything the rider asks him to. Ponies will invariably jump bigger fences out hunting or in competitions, provided they have been properly schooled, than they do at home in cold blood.

Sometimes a lead from another pony will give the necessary confidence, especially over a fence which cannot be lowered. If the animal is just idle or bored it is better to keep to low fences; wake him up by riding more vigorously and by schooling with another pony or, if old enough, take him hunting.

Lastly, there is the long whip in the hands of an assistant; this is certainly effective with some unwilling ponies, but it is apt to frighten the rider more than the pony and what is gained by the one is lost by the other. Loud shouts are to be deprecated; better to lower the fence – or change the rider.

Rushing

A keen pony is apt to develop the habit of rushing his fences. In this case he should not be schooled over a series of fences in line ahead. Rather should he be ridden in a circle close to a single fence. When he is going quietly, the circle may unobtrusively be enlarged to include the fence, which he will probably take quite calmly. If he does not, reduce the size of the circle and miss the fence until he is quiet again. (see Fig. 13, 'Fence for lungeing').

In the case of a pony who 'hots up' when he sees a course of show or schooling fences, he should be circled quietly among them until he has settled down, when the circle is varied as before to

FIGURE 27 (a).   RUSHING HIS FENCES

FIGURE 27 (b).   TAKING HIS FENCES CALMLY

include a fence. Sometimes a pony will jump more calmly at a double, which has the effect of making him look carefully and lower his head.

A frequent cause of rushing is the action of the rider in taking a pull or a tighter hold of the pony's head in front of a fence. In this case the rider must learn to keep his hands steady and not to increase the pull on the reins. It is surprising how often a loose rein will cure this fault.

Cavalletti

Six or even four cavalletti are a very useful possession. They serve a variety of purposes in the schooling of ponies and riders, and they can be used to build up many different types of jumps, e.g. a "Grid", "Parallel Bars," "In and Out," "Oxer," "Triple," "Jump with Wings." They can also be used in front of a fence, to stop ponies from rushing.

One cavalletti can be placed so as to fix the pole at 10 ins., 15 ins., or 19 ins. Extra height and spread can be obtained by building up one on top of the other. Figure 28 shows a useful method of constructing cavalletti.

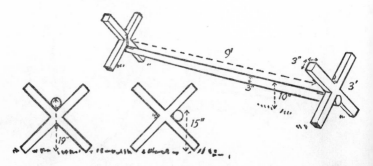

FIGURE 28.   CONSTRUCTION OF CAVALLETTI, SHOWING DIMENSIONS

The Use of Cavalletti

Value for the Rider

    (1) Gradually develops the correct position over jumps, combining balance, suppleness, style and strength.

    (2) Gives the feeling of rhythm and the ability to judge the pony's stride.

Value for the Pony

    (1) A physical exercise which develops muscles, balance, suppleness, agility, stamina and obedience.

    (2) Develops ease and rhythm of stride, with impulsion and engagement of the hindquarters.

    (3) Develops calmness and the correct technique in jumping.

Figure 45 (page 84) illustrates these benefits well.

Method of Use

Every pony needs to be introduced to the cavalletti poles gradually, so as he will always approach and negotiate them calmly, with a supple back and loin and a stretched and lowered neck.

Stage 1. At a walk. The purpose is simply to introduce the pony to the cavalletti. Start with one pole on the ground. Progress by introducing more poles, placed approximately 4 ft. to 5 ft. apart, and increase the pace to a trot for the last few strides.

Stage 2. At a trot. Start, as before, with poles on the ground, from 4 ft. to 5 ft. apart, according to the pony's stride. In some cases, with a long striding pony, they may even be placed as much as 6 ft. apart. Introduce more poles gradually, until the pony can negotiate six in a row, with lightness and regular rhythm. (See Fig. 29 left hand side).

When the pony is going calmly and rhythmically over the poles, cavalletti may be introduced, one at a time, at their lowest height

(10 inches). For ponies which rush, various alternatives can be tried. For example, when one pole has been taken quietly it may be best to put the last pole of the six down next, at a distance of about 20 to 25 feet, and then to fill in the intermediate poles.

It is important in this, as in all exercises, not to go on to the next stage until the previous stage has been practised and confirmed correctly.

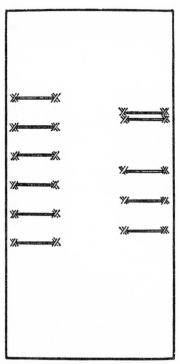

FIGURE 29.

DIAGRAM—TROTTING CAVALLETTI.   *Left*—4 FT. TO 5 FT. APART

Right—SMALL JUMP APPROXIMATELY 9 F

DISTANCE FROM LAST CAVALLETT

Stage 3. Introduce a small jump at the end of the line of, say, five cavalletti by removing pole No. 4 and placing it up against pole No. 5. (See Fig. 29 right hand side).

The jump can gradually be widened and raised in height (see Figure 30) and its precise distance from the last trotting cavalletti shortened or lengthened, according to the results required.

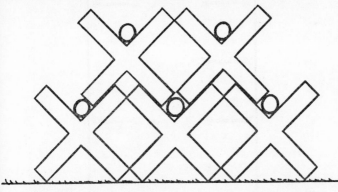

FIGURE 30. A SPREAD FENCE CONSTRUCTED FROM CAVALLETTI

Stage 4. Introduce two jumps into the line of cavalletti at approximately 9 ft. distances, by removing pole No. 2 and placing it up against pole No. 3.

Stage 5. Introduce three jumps. The time taken to reach Stage 5 is unpredictable, but it is essential to 'progress slowly' in order to maintain calmness and a correct physical development during all lessons.

The last jump can be of various designs, in order to introduce the young pony to different kinds of fences (see example in Fig. 50).

    Note. For trotting strides, the height of the cavalletti should not exceed 10 ins., or the pony will be obliged to 'hop' to negotiate them

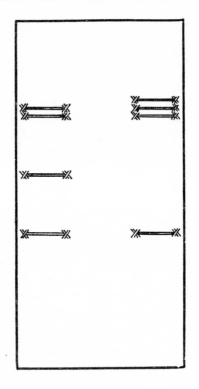

FIGURE 31.

CANTERING CAVALLETTI.   *Left*—APPROXIMATELY 9 FT. TO 10 FT. APART
                         Right—A 'DISTANCE GUIDE' 18 FT. TO 20 FT.
                         FROM FENCE

Stage 6. At a canter. Begin with one cavalletti, turned over
to the middle height (15 ins.), as a keen pony may try to jump
two at once, if the poles are too close to one another. Progress by
introducing more cavalletti, as in Stage 2, with poles, at first,
approximately 18 ft. to 20 ft. apart. Then insert cavalletti between

these, at approximately 9 ft. to 10 ft. distances, (see Fig. 31), until the pony is able to negotiate a line of poles at the canter.

The last jump may be built up, as before, and the cavalletti may be turned to their maximum height (19 ins.).

A cavalletti may be used as a 'distance guide' before a built-up fence, to help the pony to arrive at the right place for the take-off (see Fig. 31). The distance the pole is placed away from the

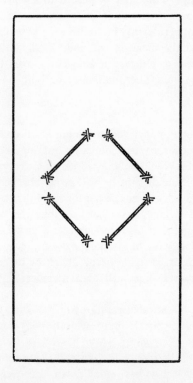

FIGURE 32. A 'BOX' OF CAVALLETTI

jump will vary according to the pony's length of stride, but approximately 18 ft. to 20 ft. may be found most suitable.

A 'Box' of Cavalletti.   (See Figure 32).

This is a useful variation to placing the cavalletti in a straight line and is excellent for developing obedience and agility. The cavalletti are placed at right-angles to one another to form a 'box', with spaces at the corners, through which the pony may pass without jumping. They may be placed to allow for one, or two strides, e.g. approximately 10 ft. or approximately 20 ft.

The pony, or the ride, may be circled round the jumps, or ridden normally round the manege, and individually called in to pass through the gaps, to jump in and out, or to pass through a gap, then jump, etc., etc. The jumps may be built-up and varied as desired.

Hunting

A well developed pony, whose training has been on sound lines, can be taken out for a very short day's hunting when he is rising four years old. He would only be ridden about very quietly at that age and shown hounds, but he will go all the better for it as a four-year old. He should not be out for more than an hour or two. There is an old saying: 'Never hot up a four-year old'. The pony is at a turning point in his career and he is growing fast. Even if all has gone well with his training he will, as a four-year old, either drop back or go right ahead. Therefore during this critical year aim at progress but with even more care, gentleness and firmness.

It may calm an excitable young pony if, on the first few occasions, he is taken out hunting with a well-mannered stable companion.

Do not over excite him or let him pull. Ride about quietly at a walk and trot. When he has settled down, encourage him to stand still if he will, but do not force him to do so; this may result in lashing out or standing up. Rather keep him quietly on the move away from others. Start him cantering on his own on a loose rein and do not encourage him to pull. Only when he will canter in this way should he be allowed to go with others. Never race other ponies. If he pulls do not put him in a stronger bit, which may spoil his mouth, but give him fewer oats, more hay and more work.

Do not overface him at this stage. Jump the sort of fences he has jumped at home, but gradually as his four-year old season progresses, the rider can give him longer days and jump bigger fences.

One afternoon, about the Christmas holidays, when people have begun to go home and the country is no longer 'blind', the pony may be allowed to 'have a go', cantering quietly and freely after the hounds and, if possible, jumping fences in his own place and without a lead. After this he will quickly gain experience, but he must not be overtaxed or the youthful physical ailments (splints, curbs, etc.) will appear all too soon.

FIGURE 33. JUMPING HIS OWN PLACE WITHOUT A LEAD

STAGE III

Basic training: aims and objects

If the rider takes a great deal of trouble in the initial stages of training, he will reap great benefits as time goes on because, in order to be a good ride, a pony must go correctly in all paces. The system of training recommended here will benefit all ponies and is essential for those that are being trained for combined training events.

Our aim and object is that the pony should learn what is necessary in order to be a good, all round riding pony and hunter.

The pony should go freely forward with an even cadence. He must be 'on the bit' at all paces. He must have a steady, correct head-carriage, be in balance, straight, supple and completely obedient to the rider's aids.

Let us consider how these aims can be achieved. It is wishful thinking to imagine that this high standard of training can be achieved in a short time. It is not possible, and any short cut taken by the use of auxiliary reins, etc., will show itself in many different ways. Any restriction or force used will result in shortened paces and, more than likely, incorrect head-carriage. For instance, should the rider use a martingale in order to hold the pony's head down, having it so fitted that the pony can 'lean' against it, the pony will be using the wrong muscles in his neck and will miss it the moment it is removed. Consequently he will throw up his head, feeling for the strap which is not there, all of which will have aggravated a fault which will take long to correct.

If a young pony is inclined to throw his head up into a dangerous position, it is advisable to use a standing martingale, properly fitted so that it only comes into action when the pony has thrown his head up beyond the point of control. Fitted in this way, it acts only as a safeguard for the rider and in no way hinders the pony's training. The use of a running martingale for this purpose is unwise, as it influences the reins and causes a false action on the pony's mouth.

The rider must plan the schooling of his pony and the plan must be strictly adhered to. It is most important that the pony should become proficient in one stage before taken on to the next. This point must be stressed, because the pony has to learn to know what the aids mean. If great care is taken to make the aids clear and correct, the pony will soon learn what is wanted of him; but if he is hurried and the aids are not clear, he will get muddled, hot up and go back in his training.

Cadence

A pony must learn to stand still when being mounted. It should be the first lesson in obedience and the rider must be very strict about this. He should get off every time the pony moves, remount, and only give the aid to move on when the pony has stood perfectly still.

The pony must learn to go forward to the slightest pressure of the rider's leg aid. If at first the pony does not respond, the rider can use a fairly long switch with which to touch him behind the girth, at the same time as he gives the leg aid to 'go forward'. The pony will soon learn this aid and when he will go forward to the lightest pressure of the rider's legs, the stick need no longer be used.

The pony should trot forward at a brisk, controlled pace, with as long a stride as possible. Should he at any time quicken his pace, he must be brought back to a slower pace and then be asked again gradually to lengthen his stride (see Fig. 34). Each time he quickens or loses cadence, the pace must be reduced and the exercise repeated. The amount of forward impulsion created should be determined by the temperament of the pony. Whereas the free-going pony would probably go naturally forward with long strides, the slow, lazy pony will need to be kept going forward by the use of the rider's legs and seat. The rider must at all times maintain a light, smooth and even contact with the pony's mouth.

At this stage the correct head-carriage will involve the neck being long and stretched and the head being in front of the perpendicular.

FIGURE 34.   LENGTHENING THE STRIDE

Positioning the head

We must now study how to get the pony's head in the correct position. If the pony carries his head too high he must be 'asked' to bring it down. Nothing is gained by the use of force, because the moment the force is relaxed the head will once more take the false, high position. Most ponies are stiffer on one side than the other, which means they resist more to one side than they do to the other. Therefore they are slightly more bent one way, because the muscles are shorter on the side to which they are bent than on the other side. In order to get the pony going straight, the muscles on the short (soft) side must be lengthened, so as to be the same as those on the resisting side.

(1). THE PONY ANSWERING THE REIN ON THE 'SOFT' SIDE

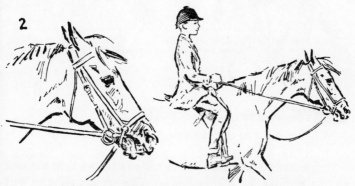

(2). THE PONY RESISTING THE REIN ON THE 'HARD' SIDE

FIGURE 35. FINDING THE PONY'S STIFF SIDE

In order to ascertain which is the stiff side, the rider should walk the horse on a loose rein, then pick up the left rein only (see Fig. 35, No. 1) and if the pony answers immediately by turning his head to the left and moving off in that direction, it is almost certain that this is the soft side. If the rider now drops the left rein and picks up the right rein and he finds that the pony will not turn his head to the right but moves in that direction with a stiff jaw and neck, keeping his head straight or even turning it slightly to the left (see Fig. 35, No. 2), then the right side is the stiff side. Having established this fact, the rider sets about 'asking' the pony to lower his head (if it is too high) and relax his jaw.

FIGURE 36.   THE PONY MUST BE 'ASKED' TO LOWER HIS HEAD

He proceeds at the trot as described and takes a light but firm contact with the left rein (soft side). This contact must be kept throughout the lesson, no matter in what direction he is going. Now, by a slight tightening and relaxing of the fingers on the right rein (stiff side) the rider 'asks' for a relaxation of the pony's jaw and a consequent lowering of the head (see Fig. 36). The motion is like 'squeezing-water-out-of-a-sponge' and must not in any way be backwards.   At the same time as the rider 'asks' with his right hand, he also uses his legs, the right leg giving a stronger aid than the left. If this is repeated every time the pony gets his head too high, he will soon learn to lower it and relax his jaw (see Fig. 36). If the horse is stiff on the left side the aids are, of course, reversed.

In the case of too low a head-carriage, the rider must use his legs to push the pony's head up, by making the hind legs more active (see Fig. 37). The rider must never attempt to pull the head up with his hands, as the result would be a false head-carriage, with the top of the neck bent in a concave position, which is very damaging to the training. Carrying the head up in this position has the effect of hollowing the pony's back and thus making it impossible for him to use his back correctly or to bring his hind legs under him. While the rider is teaching his pony to hold his head correctly, he must also concentrate on getting him into the habit of keeping it in this position when changing direction or altering pace. He must also remember to keep his pony trotting on in the same cadence, with a long stride.

1   *2*

FIGURE 37. THE RIDER MUST 'PUSH' THE PONY'S HEAD UP

A pony is a creature of habit. He nearly always does the same thing in the same place. It is the artist who understands this and can anticipate a fault, correcting it before it has in fact appeared.

Position of the head during transitions

At this stage, the pony must be asked to reduce his pace from trot to walk very carefully and slowly. If he is hurried in any way, up will go the head again with the same false bend of the neck, causing a great deal of resistance in the mouth and back; or he might just catch hold of the bit and 'lie' on it. In order to get a smooth reduction of pace, the rider closes both legs, sits very deep in the saddle, whilst he lightly resists with the hands and 'asks' with the right hand and right leg (in this case), for a relaxation of the jaw; as the pony responds, the rider must instantaneously be still with his hands and gently push the pony into a walk with his legs. The secret lies in 'asking' and rewarding by the *immediate* relaxation of the aid when the pony has responded.

From a walk, the pony must be brought back to a halt, using exactly the same aids as when going from a trot into a walk. It is important for the pony to be made to stand squarely, equally balanced on all four legs. If one hind leg is left behind, the rider can gently tap this leg with a switch, while giving a gentle aid with his leg on the same side. The pony will gradually learn to answer and bring up the hind leg the moment he is asked. This will soon become a habit and he will adopt this stance on his own. It is sometimes difficult to feel which hind leg is left behind, without looking down. As a guide, one should remember that whichever fore leg is the last to move, it will be the opposite hind leg which will need to be moved up. The pony must stand perfectly still until given the aid to move forward.

Practically every pony will alter the position of his head or change the length of his stride when changing direction or pace. The intelligent rider will anticipate this by preparing the pony for a change. He 'asks' on the stiff side with this hand and leg *before* changing direction or pace, as much as to say: 'Pay attention, I am going to do something different'.

Until the pony will go forward with a level stride at a trot, change direction, and come back to a walk without resisting or throwing up his head, he must not be taken on to the next stage. Large circles may be ridden but still the rider must demand nothing more than a level pace, a light mouth and to go forward to the leg aids.

The canter

The pony should now be ready to learn to strike off into a canter. As the canter is a pace of three-time, the 'laterals' on the side to which he is cantering (that is, the leading fore leg and the hind leg on the same side) are slightly in advance of the other fore leg and hind leg, and therefore the pony should be slightly bent towards his leading fore leg. If he is bent correctly going round a left-hand corner (which means he is slightly curved to the left) and then given the aids to canter by the rider drawing back his right leg and creating a strong pressure with *both* legs, seat and back muscles, the pony will go quite naturally into a left canter. It is important here to draw particular attention to the use of *both* the rider's legs, together with the seat and back muscles. A pony will very quickly learn this aid. If the rider gets slack about using the aid correctly and eventually just brings back his leg, together with the use of the opposite rein, he will find himself in difficulties when, in the future training, he wants to teach his pony lateral work. The aids being much the same, the rider must make himself very clear to his pony, or he will find that on asking for a half-pass the pony goes into a canter.

In the early stages the canter should be brisk and long, without collection, but with the same light contact with the pony's mouth. Should the pony start to 'lie' on the bit, he must be given a half-halt by a strong use of the rider's back, seat, and leg aids and then allowed to continue. If he puts up any resistance to one side, the same 'giving-and-taking' movement can be applied with the rein on the 'stiff' side, as has been described previously. If there is no particular resistance to one side or the other, but just a general 'lying on the bit', the 'giving-and-taking' hand should be the one on the opposite side to the leading leg.

Only if the pony's hind legs are active is it possible to get a balanced pony 'sitting' on his hocks at the canter. Here again it is important to stress the tremendous power of the rider's back aid. By straightening the back, together with a slight resistance of the hands, the rider can push the pony's hind legs under him by lowering the haunches. This should be done gradually, until the pony will take up the position on his own account and become lightly balanced, while cantering on freely. With practice, the rider will come to feel the pony relaxing his back muscles, and the moment this happens he must sit still until he feels the back hard and resisting again. Then he must repeat the aid until gradually the pony remains cantering in a soft, relaxed position.

In order to bring the pony quietly back to a trot from a canter, the rider straightens his spine while resisting slightly with the hand on the 'soft' side and 'asking' with the other hand. This transition should be practised continually so as to get it smooth, with no resistance or upward movement of the pony's head. Gradually it will be found that the moment the rider sits deep, closes his legs, and 'asks' with the hand on the stiff side, the pony will come straight back into a correct trot stride and continue with a soft mouth, without any more resistance from the reins being necessary.

Placing the pony 'on the bit'

The pony should now be ready to be put 'on the bit' and to stay on it. Up to now we have only asked for a relaxation of the jaw and that the pony should go with a very light contact with the bit. Now, using the same methods as before (i.e., the 'squeezing-water-out-of-a-sponge' movement whenever a resistance is put up) the pony must be made not only to relax the jaw but to hold the bit softly in his mouth with a light contact and remain in this position at all paces and in all directions.

In order to trot correctly the pony must 'swing' his back and be active with his hind legs. Unless he can do this, it is impossible for him to get round a corner smoothly or to perform a circle correctly. When making a circle, the pony's inside lateral legs must take a shorter stride than the outside laterals. If he is stiff and does not use his back, he cannot bend his hocks enough to keep the hind feet following exactly the imprints made by the fore feet. Therefore he throws them out and they perform a larger circle than the fore legs.

Suppling the pony

To overcome this the rider can supple his pony by means of various exercises. To supple the pony from front to rear, he performs a series of half-halts, obtained in the same manner as described previously when coming from a trot to a walk; only in this case the pony is asked to trot on again just before breaking into a walk. The best method of suppling a pony laterally is to perform a shoulder-in. The importance of this exercise is that the pony must bend his spine, and by so doing flex his hocks, which can then be brought more underneath him. It is useless if he bends his neck only, which is undoubtedly what he will try to do. Because he finds it difficult to bend at the spine, he will try to create the illusion that he is doing so by bending his neck only, and thus evade the exercise. This will do more harm than good, because if he is allowed to make this evasion he will, in time, become what is called 'rubber-necked'. The term is self explanatory and the fault very difficult to correct.

To perform a right shoulder-in, the pony's forehand is taken off the track as if about to start a circle, but instead of continuing the circle the rider's inside (right) leg, held at the girth, pushes the pony's forehand to the left, so that the pony will continue going forward with the head, neck and spine following a curve of which the centre is the rider's right leg. At the same time the rider keeps the pony's hind legs on the track and his quarters from going to the left by bringing his left leg back behind the girth, thus controlling the quarters and maintaining the impulsion. (see Fig. 38).

The easiest way to start a shoulder-in is on a bend. Coming round the corner, the rider applies the above aids and, instead of straightening out after the corner, he holds this position. If the pony responds by performing just two steps sideways, the pressure of the inside leg should immediately be relaxed and the pony allowed to go forward into a large half-circle. It is better to continue on a circle than to bring the forehand back on to the track, because the pony being already bent in the direction of the circle, should be allowed to do the easiest movement as a reward for having responded to the aid. Very gradually, the pony must be asked to do more and more steps at the shoulder-in until he will perform this exercise to either hand, for quite long stretches, with the greatest of ease.

This exercise is best performed at a trot, but sometimes it is easier to teach the pony to understand the aids, at first, at a walk. However, as soon as the pony understands what is required of him, it should not be performed at a walk again. The better the movement, the better the exercise and it is dangerous to do too much work at the walk, except on a long rein, as the pony will lose impulsion and can more easily produce evasions and get behind the bit.

There can be different degrees of shoulder-in. It is better to get the pony moving on two different tracks so that, while the hind legs continue on one track, the fore legs follow a line parallel to them (see right shoulder-in, Fig. 38), because in this way the rider will get more flexibility of the spine and more activity in the hind legs. At first the rider can ask for only a small bend, so that the inside hind leg follows the track made by the outside fore leg;

FIGURE 38. RIGHT SHOULDER-IN

but the rider must be quite certain that the pony is in this position and not just bending his neck. No force must be used in this exercise and it must not be performed if the pony's head is too high. The head and neck must remain still and in the correct position. To perform the left shoulder-in, the aids are reversed.

In order to appreciate the importance of the shoulder-in as a suppling exercise, it should be realised that it is the easiest way in which to make a pony straight, because it makes him bend his spine on the stiff side and activates the hind legs, which otherwise he would not attempt to do.

Circles

It is now time to ask for more correctness in the pony's movements. To ride a circle correctly, the pony's spine should comply with the direction of the movement and follow the circumference of the circle. It is easy for a spectator to see if a pony is correct or not, because hind feet should follow exactly in the tracks made by the fore feet. They may be on or over them, according to the pace at which the pony is going, but not to one side or the other. It has been made clear why it is so necessary to ask only large circles during the early stages of training. The smaller the circle the more active must be the hind legs, in order that they bend enough to follow the tracks made by the fore feet.

FIGURE 39.
THE PONY MUST CHANGE THE BEND AS HE CHANGES DIRECTION

It is interesting to assess the progress and accuracy of the training by riding a circle on ground upon which the imprints of the pony's hoofs can be seen.

A pony must always look to the way he is going (except in the shoulder-in). If performing a circle to the right, he must be bent in a curve round the rider's right leg, and if going to the left, he must be bent round the left leg (see Fig. 39). A pony should follow the direction in which his head is pointing. That is why it is so necessary to be as accurate as possible when riding through corners during the early stages of training.

The rider must be careful to see that the pony remains on the bit during the whole circle. Any exercise incorrectly performed should be repeated again and again until it is done correctly. Then make much of the pony before continuing with another exercise, or give him a rest by walking on a long rein.

The rider

One cannot lay down any hard or fast rule for training a pony and this is only meant as a guide. Some ponies take much longer than others, so it is impossible to give any specific time. But if the work so far has been correct, the pony should by now be permanently 'on the bit', which means he is holding it lightly in his mouth, with a relaxed jaw, and obeying the aids without resistance. Naturally there will always be moments when the pony puts up an evasion and resists the bit, but he should respond immediately to a correction given. If he does not obey and if there is no obvious reason like excitement, caused by another pony, a car going down the road, or a bird suddenly flying up, then the rider must ask himself why, and what has been wrong with his training. It may be that he uses too much hand and not enough leg. It may be that he is stiff himself, which will communicate itself at once to the pony, with dire results. Or it may be that he has not been clear enough with his aids.

It is very important for the rider to analyse himself and to be sure he is sitting correctly. If he is getting too far forward, he will not be in a position to give correct aids. If he is sitting in the shape of a bow, it would be impossible for him to use his back to push the pony forward. If he loses his temper he will never get anywhere. So, if things go wrong, the rider must not blame the pony but himself, and correct his position if necessary.

Every day the rider must go over all these exercises we have discussed. As time goes on, he must ask for a better and better performance, aiming always towards perfection. He must be more strict with the not-so-good movements. If the rider is satisfied with the progress his pony has made, he may now take his training on a further step by teaching him to counter-canter.

The counter-canter

This is also an excellent suppling exercise, but it must not be attempted too early as, until the pony is fairly supple he canno' perform it correctly and he will start changing legs behind, which is a very difficult habit to cure.

First try rather long and not very deep loops (serpentine) at the canter.   For instance, canter in a school or alongside a fence on the right leg; then bring the pony off the track and return to the track without changing legs. The rider must remember to keep the pony bent to the right, even when going to the left, as it is important for him to keep the bend towards the leading leg. As the pony gets more and more supple, these serpentines can get deeper and deeper, until the rider can take his pony round a school in a counter-canter and finally perform a complete circle. (This means going round to the left with the right leg leading, or vice versa). Progress must be very gradual, and the rider must be content with a little at a time. It is far better to go slowly and get it right, than to hurry in the early stages and then later have to correct other faults which have been produced by 'forcing the pace' Naturally, the exercise must be practised equally on both reins.

The counter-canter must not be confused with the disunited canter, which is an evasion and is always incorrect. In the true canter, one pair of laterals (both legs on one side) should be in advance of the other pair (see page 32, under the heading 'The canter'). In the disunited canter the pony is leading with the near-fore and the off-hind, or vice versa.

The walk from the canter

The next exercise to teach the pony is the canter-to-walk. This must only be attempted if the rider is quite sure the pony will answer his seat aids and relax his back muscles, by producing more active hock action. If the pony is at all stiff in the back, the rider will not be able to get a correct canter-to-walk and much resistance and throwing up of the pony's head will result, all of which will be very detrimental to the pony's training.

It is best to start this movement on a fairly large circle, as the pony finds it easier to be balanced at the canter when not on a straight line. The rider closes his legs, sits very deep and well down in the saddle and, by using strong seat and back aids, supported by closed legs into resisting hands, pushes the pony's hind legs more and more underneath him, until the pony's balance is such that he can pass straight into a walk. This will not be accomplished the first time it is attempted, because it is probable that the pony will not be sufficiently in balance by being too strong on the bit, and will therefore have to take two or three steps at a trot. If the rider's aids are not clear or strong enough, the pony will come back with his weight on his forehand. The rider must make the pony canter more and more slowly by lowering the croup, and thus making him light in hand. Only then can the pony pass straight into a walk. As soon as the pony walks, the reins must immediately be relaxed and the pony allowed to walk freely on without any restriction.

The simple change

When the foregoing movement has been successfully achieved, the rider may attempt a simple change of leg, but it is most important to get the canter-to-walk first. It is also necessary before starting this exercise, to be sure that the pony will strike off into a canter on either leg on a straight line and be perfectly straight while doing so. It would be a mistake to try a simple change of leg if the pony throws his quarters in when striking off into a canter, as it would only aggravate this fault and then there would be many difficulties to overcome in order to get a correct change of leg. The reason for correct canter aids is now obvious. If the rider's inside leg and seat are used to the same extent as the outside leg, the pony will not learn this annoying habit of pushing his quarters to the inside when striking off into a canter, and there will be no need for any corrections.

To practise the simple change of leg at the canter: canter off on a named leg, perform a canter-to-walk and walk on for some distance before striking off on the other leg. Gradually reduce the length of walk in between the canters until there are only two or three paces at the walk. The resulting simple change of leg will have been performed with the greatest of ease.

This is the correct simple change of leg; but in all dressage tests up to Medium class this change can be done progressively through a trot. There must, however, always be a few paces performed at the walk.

Conclusion

If this system of training is carefully adhered to, so that all resistance is reduced to a minimum before any difficult exercise is asked, the rider will find these exercises falling into his lap, like a ripe plum does from a tree, directly the pony understands what is required of him. Because, having taught the pony obedience and how to relax, the rider does not have the dual task of teaching him simultaneously a new aid, and overcoming a resistance. The secret is obedience – the proud result of correct training, which has caused the pony to give himself willingly and to obey, with pleasure, the indications of the rider. This training will have developed the pony's muscles and suppled him to such an extent as to make jumping easier. It will also have got him into the habit of obedience, which will go a long way towards eliminating the possibility of refusals when jumping.

STAGE IV

More advanced training

The object at this stage is to bring the training of the pony up to a high standard.

He should be keen and responsive but obedient, submissive and relaxed. He should be on the bit, with a steady head-carriage, and must 'carry himself'; he must not throw his head, snatch at the bit or pull. He should go on a loose rein at all paces when required to.

Everything must be done to develop freedom of movement and action, more extension, greater smoothness, suppleness and straightness. Regular cadence and rhythm must be confirmed.

The trained pony should jump all kinds of fences at all paces, temperately and in good style. He should go kindly alone or in company and he should have good manners.

The pony should reach this stage at about five years old, providing he has been correctly trained from the start.

Previous training – especially the basic training – must be continued, confirmed and improved. Longer strides and brisker action in the extended paces and smaller circles (10 yards diameter at the canter) should be achieved. Practice the counter-canter, serpentine (3 yards on either side of a straight line) at the canter without change of leg, walk from the canter and the simple change (canter-walk-canter). For these exercises the pony must be relaxed, obedient and offer no resistance, keeping his head steady and the rider, as always, should be relaxed, calm and definite with his aids. As soon as he does what is asked of him, the pony must immediately be rewarded, and there must be plenty of loose rein work. As a guide, especially for the impatient trainer, there should be as much extended and loose rein work as 'collected' work.

Further school movements which should now be started include:

Turn on the haunches (Half Pirouette)

Once the rider has control of the pony's quarters by means of the turn on the forehand, he may start to teach the turn on the haunches. This can be executed at the walk, trot or canter; with the young pony, especially one which will proceed to more advanced work, it is not advisable to practice this movement at the halt as once the fixed pivot has been learned it is difficult to teach the pony to maintain the cadence. Start by making a small circle with the hind legs, maintaining the pace of the walk.

To turn to the right the rider leads the forehand round with the right rein supported by the left; the left leg acting behind the girths prevents the quarters going to the left while the right leg, at the girth, maintains impulsion and keeps the pony from stepping back. The left foreleg should pass in front of the right and the left hindleg acts similarly; the pony should turn smoothly, maintaining the exact rhythm.

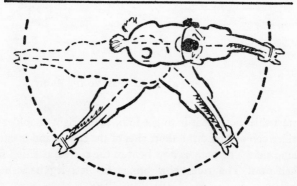

FIGURE 40. TURN ON THE HAUNCHES

Lateral work: the half pass

The rider has now got his pony supple; his cadence is established, his head is steady and he accepts the bit, so lateral work can be commenced. A pony normally moves on one track, that is to say the track made by the hind legs follows exactly that made by the fore legs. When the pony is asked to move sideways, the track made by the hind legs is separate from that made by the fore legs, and he moves to one side or the other on two tracks. The easiest way to

FIGURE 41.   HALF PASS TO THE RIGHT

start this movement is to get into, say, a right shoulder-in as the rider comes round the short side of the school and is entering the long side. The pony is now bent in the correct position for a right half pass. The rider now brings his left leg back behind the girths and, as he releases the action of his right leg, the pony will move forward and to the right, but the inside leg must then be used to keep up the forward impulsion.

An alternative way of starting lateral work is to perform a half-circle and, with the use of the drawn-back outside leg, the pony is

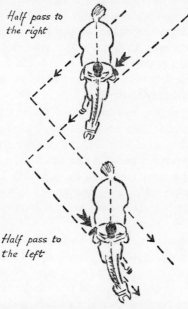

Half pass to the right

Half pass to the left

FIGURE 42. HALF PASS TO THE RIGHT
HALF PASS TO THE LEFT

brought back to the side of the school on two tracks, again with the aid of the inside leg.

This movement may also be carried out on the open road when the pony is going freely, perhaps towards home. Using the aids described above, the pony will perform the half pass across the road.

At this stage it is not of vast importance to keep the correct bend. A forced head-carriage will always end in producing stiffness, resistance and a loss of cadence. But as the pony learns to go away from the rider's leg, the trainer must then get stricter in maintaining the correct bend, which should be slightly looking in the direction to which he is moving. The legs on the side to which the pony is bent or moving are known as the 'inside legs', whilst those on the other side are called the 'outside legs'. The pony's outside legs should cross over in front of the inside legs and his body should be parallel to the side of the school. He must maintain his cadence and free forward movement and on no account must he be allowed to shorten his stride.

When first teaching this movement the rider must be very careful that the pony does not dive away, throwing his weight on his forehand, when taking the first steps on two tracks. This is the usual evasion produced and it is one which must be overcome at once, and more activity created in the haunches, before the movement is attempted again. Only one or two side steps should be asked for at the beginning and, as these improve, more can be attempted.

This is a movement which proves whether the pony will go away from the rider's legs in a lateral direction, and it is often required in all practical riding. Furthermore, it is an excellent exercise for suppling the pony and is required in dressage tests to show the obedience of the horse to the rider's hands and legs.

The rein-back

It is not good to ask a pony to rein-back too often, as it may encourage him to get behind the bit and, when asked to 'stand still', he might start anticipating the rein-back. Although it is important for him to know how to rein-back, it should be practised carefully and the trainer must be sure that it is performed correctly.

FIGURE 43. REIN BACK—RIGHT AND WRONG

The rider brings his pony to a halt and, whilst his legs are still acting, the hands resist so the pony, finding he cannot go forwards, goes backwards due to the impulsion created by the leg aids. Having learnt to answer the rein-aid on his stiff side, the pony will now rein back quite easily if the rider 'asks' with this rein at the same time as he 'asks' for the rein-back. The pace is in two-time. He must rein-back by lifting each diagonal pair at the same time.

He must not be pulled back, or he will throw up his head and hollow his back so that he could not step backwards correctly. He must keep his head still and step back perfectly straight.

Training tests

By this time the pony should be capable of doing the Pony Club Tests.

The object of these elementary training tests is to encourage progressive training of both pony and rider. All tests aim at simplifying the pony's and rider's task, in order that the pony may develop quietly and happily. In preparing for these tests, great care must be taken that the pony does not become routined. If the whole test is performed day after day the pony will anticipate the movements and perform them before any 'aid' is given. In training, therefore, it is advisable to vary the order of the movements constantly and the places where they are performed.

The double bridle

If satisfactory progress has been made and the pony is balanced, on the bit, and can carry out the ordinary movements correctly while ridden in a snaffle, the double bridle may be introduced. It must not be used because the pony's head-carriage in a snaffle is incorrect, nor because he pulls. If this is done it will lead to a hard or spoiled mouth and a shortening of the stride. When the pony is ready for it, the double bridle will improve his head-carriage and

add to his action and performance. The rider will find no difficulty when the pony is put in a double bridle provided he has
been taught to go correctly in a snaffle.

The double bridle consists of a bridoon, which is a snaffle, a
curb-bit and a curb-chain. Its function is:

(a) The bridoon acts in the same way as a jointed
snaffle.

(b) The curb can act at the same time as the bridoon
to give a more refined and imperceptible aid and
to help to maintain a relaxed jaw.

The bridoon should lie in the pony's mouth as high as possible
without causing the lips to wrinkle; the curb bit should lie immediately below it. The curb chain, which should be thick and
flat, should lie snugly in the chin groove and be sufficiently tight
to allow the cheek pieces of the bit to be drawn back to an angle
of 45 degrees with the pony's mouth.

The mouthpiece presses on the bars and the tongue; the cheeks
of the bit act as a lever to increase the pressure on the bars; the
curb chain is the fulcrum and should be painless.

The bit should be sufficiently wide so that the cheeks do not
pinch the pony's lips ; a thick mouthpiece is milder than a thin
one ; a long cheek is a more powerful lever and therefore more
severe than a short one. A high port can be painful and is not
recommended, but if a port is used it should be high enough and
wide enough to allow the tongue to fit snugly underneath it.

For a young pony, a mild bit with a thick mouthpiece, a tongue
groove and a medium or short cheek is recommended. It is important that the double bridle should be very carefully fitted.

When ridden in a double bridle, the pony must be on the bit
and relaxed in his movements. He must not open his jaws or
throw the bit about in his mouth. He should bend at the poll but

the line of his face must not come back behind the perpendicular.
In fact he should go in exactly the same way as when in a snaffle
bridle with, possibly, more brilliance.

FIGURE 44.   THE DOUBLE BRIDLE

The double bridle is not a bit for the inexperienced rider
because great damage can be done by its misuse, and it is not
good for a young pony, because it would restrict his action if used

before he understood how to accept the bit. It is important for the rider to hold the snaffle rein on the outside, so that more contact can be taken on this rein than on the curb rein, which should only be used with a very light contact.

Jumping

All types of fences should now be jumped, alone and in company. Fences should be wider, larger and more varied. As many spread as upright fences should be used and water jumps of some sort should be taken every day.

Include show fences up to a maximum of 3 ft. for ponies of 14.2 h.h. or over as well as the type of jumps met with in hunter trials and horse trials. Smaller ponies should be schooled over smaller fences. (As a guide, lower the fence by an inch for every inch of the pony's height).

Associates riding larger ponies and horses may wish to teach them to jump faster with a view to riding them in point-to-points or horse trials. When a horse will jump fast alone he may be schooled in company, with a view to sharpening him up and getting him used to going with others.

At this stage the pony should be jumping freely and in good style with emphasis on smooth approach, steady head-carriage and free use of the head, neck and loins.

Do not go on jumping fences over and over again. When the pony is jumping freely and well, stop on a good note before any trouble starts, and reward the pony.

Throughout his jumping training, the pony must be absolutely obedient and jump, with pleasure, whatever the rider asks him to. Hence the importance, which cannot be over emphasized, of schooling over small and varied fences. Training on the lines already described will have developed the pony's muscles and suppled him to such an extent as to make jumping easier. He will also have learnt the habit of obedience, which will go a long way towards eliminating the possibility of refusals.

FIGURE 45.   OBEDIENCE

Hunting

Continue on the same lines as in the previous stage and the season before. A good five-year-old pony should be able to go out for two short days a week. This is much better than one long day, which may tire and overtax his muscles and cause physical or other trouble.

He should be improving and gaining experience, and be capable of taking on anything that other ponies can, and of jumping in front and exactly where his rider puts him.

Care should be taken not to overtax the pony or make him pull. He should gallop smoothly and, even at this pace, go with a loose rein; he must not be allowed to race other ponies and horses in the crowd, or his mouth may well be spoilt.

He must stand still and alone and take no notice of whip or

hound. He must also stand still for his rider to open gates and hold them open for hounds, huntsman or others.

He must be quiet to box and unbox and have good manners in the hunting field.

It will be good training for the pony if he has the chance to bring on tail hounds and to go on to the corner of a covert to view the fox away. Perhaps he will get away alone with hounds and give his owner a ride which will prove that all the thought, time and trouble spent on his training have been amply repaid.

FIGURE 46.
ALONE WITH HOUNDS—WORTH ALL THE TIME AND TROUBLE

SPECIALIZED TRAINING

If the training of the pony has proceeded satisfactorily and he has reached the standards laid down for this stage, he may be given more specialized training.

In the following pages are suggestions as to how the trainer should proceed in various branches of equitation and schooling.

ELEMENTARY DRESSAGE

Forward, forward, forward! That is what a trainer must have in his mind when commencing to school a pony. He must 'go forward' into every movement, even into a halt or a rein-back. Possibly it is the most important thing for him always to keep in mind.

It is also necessary for the rider to study his own seat. The more correct it is the easier will it be for the pony to carry himself in balance and equilibrium. If the rider keeps his legs well away from the pony's sides and then suddenly applies them when an aid is required, he will surprise his pony who will consequently jump into the movement asked, instead of 'oiling' into it with grace and ease. If he sits to one side or allows his hands to move about, it will distract the pony, who will most certainly find some sort of evasion to counteract the unsteadiness of his rider.

So, trainer, first look to yourself and be sure you are sitting correctly in the middle of your saddle with a straight but supple back, firm but soft hands, and still but active legs held close to the pony's sides. And, if things go wrong, say: 'What have I done wrong' rather than blame your pony for not complying with your wishes.

When first your pony comes out in the morning it is good to walk on a long rein for several minutes and then let him go along at a nice even trot with a long neck and the head carried a little low, but not of course, overbent. His paces must not be hurried and, before starting any exercises, he should be allowed to un-limber himself with a canter round the field on a long rein. Having stretched his limbs and loosened himself up, work can then begin.

The trainer must make plans for his pony and draw up a schedule of what work he requires. He must study the nature of his pony, as some work willingly and can do more in a day than others who dislike work and take to it badly. A pony must never be pushed too far nor too fast. It is better to underwork rather than overwork him, and when he has been obedient, let him walk on a long rein and caress him to show him how good he has been. It is a great mistake to repeat a well-learnt lesson over and over again without any respite. If the pony is petted and made much of after he has been obedient he soon learns what is required of him. The lesson can go on being repeated should he not obey, followed by immediate relaxation the moment the aim has been achieved.

It is of great importance for both pony and rider to be calm. If the pony gets excited, the lesson should be changed to something easier and, when equilibrium is once more established, the former lesson may be repeated, but once more abandoned should the pony show signs of hotting up again. When the pony is calm he is willing to listen and obey his rider, should he understand what is required of him. But the moment he becomes excited all his muscles are tensed up, his back becomes stiff, and either he does not obey the aids or he does so in a very jerky, hard and uncomfortable way which is both horrid to sit on and unpleasant to watch. It is equally important for the rider to be calm. Should he lose his temper or get excited he will, without doubt, upset his pony. Should this occur it is better to stop work and walk on a long rein, or even pack up and go home and take him out again later in the day, rather than to frighten or disturb the pony.

First the pony must accept the bit and hold it softly in his mouth; the neck should be long with the head in front of the perpendicular and it must remain in this position when changing direction or altering pace. If the rider feels a resistance in the mouth he must 'play' with the rein on that side whilst applying the leg on the same side, and continue doing so till the pony 'gives' his jaw and is once more soft when the rider's hands must be quite still.

Half-halts, halts and rein-back are good exercises if carried out correctly, but devastating if the pony is pulled back by the reins and so falls on to his forehand. He must be 'pushed' into a slower pace by the use of the rider's back, thighs and legs, with the hands strong but *soft*, resisting but *not* hard. When the pony learns to come back into a half-halt with a soft back and lowered haunches, the rider can try a halt from a trot. After this is achieved, the pony can be taught to rein-back. First from a walk to halt and rein-back and then from a trot.

The rein-back is a balancing exercise and only one stride should be asked at first, then two, then three and so on, but this exercise must not be overdone nor must the pony be allowed to run back out of hand with his head stuck out in front madly resisting the bit. In this way he would just learn bad habits. He must go back in two-time, still with a light mouth and no resistance. When this is achieved it will be found to be an excellent exercise.

In the canter the pony must always be straight up and not lean inwards when changing direction or performing a circle. The beat should be three-time, and even. If the pony is relaxed it is a wonderful pace and the rider should sit very straight and still with his legs just 'stroking' the horse's sides. Should the pony tend to fall inwards or throw out his quarters during a circle, the rider should hold the inside rein firmly whilst 'asking' with the outside rein held slightly higher; at the same time he should apply the inside leg at the girths and he will find that the pony comes back into a balanced and more collected position.

When coming back to a trot from a canter, the trainer must be careful to push his pony so that he goes softly and gracefully *forwards* into a correct trot. If there should be any resistance in the pony's mouth and back, the rider must not ask for a transition until he is going softly again. He must remember never to ask a new exercise or difference in pace whilst the pony shows any kind of resistance. The same applies when coming back from a trot to a walk, or from a walk to a halt.

Finally remember, to be successful, the trainer must produce a pony who looks as if he is doing everything himself. He must be balanced, graceful, proud and willingly submit to the demands of his master. And the true artist is he who sees beauty in rhythm and tempers his will with understanding in a real partnership between himself and his pony.

FIGURE 47.   DRESSAGE TEST

APPENDIX B

SHOW JUMPING

Many Pony Club members want their ponies to take part in jumping competitions, first perhaps in hunter trials and, later, in horse trials or show jumping events.

Qualities of a show jumper

It may be well to consider the qualities to be looked for in a show jumper. He must obviously like jumping and jump with boldness and freedom. He should be active and supple, particularly in the neck, back and loins, and if he naturally folds his legs up well he will start with a great advantage. He must dislike hitting fences and should cover a lot of ground when jumping. He should have natural balance and a sense of stride when jumping loose.

Temperamentally he must have great courage and, though keen and free, must be calm. He must be receptive and willing. With regard to breeding, a pony with quality will, as a general rule, show greater courage and more powers of endurance than a commoner animal and will be far more inspiring to ride – although he may take longer to train.

Conformation is even more a matter of opinion, but it is desirable for the pony to have a well shaped and powerful hind leg, with particular emphasis on the hocks, and strength in the loins and quarters. Plenty of room in the jowl is also important so that the head and neck position is adjustable.

The objective

The trainer's objective is a trained pony which can and will jump any reasonably sized show fence cleanly, with zest, freedom and courage. He aims at being able to ride his pony smoothly throughout a round, maintaining balance at all times so that the approaches to the fences are fluent and harmonious and changes of direction accurate and suitable for his plan of riding the course.

He requires the balance to be fluid, in order that the pace can be increased or decreased to suit different types of fences, and he will need to be able to lengthen or shorten the pony's stride in order to perfect the approaches. He will expect his pony to be obedient and handy and to have good manners in the ring. He must at all times be able to maintain impulsion and to create more if circumstances demand it. The fundamental factor in all this is balance.

The trainer reaches his objective by progressive and systematic training (dressage). It will be necessary to work to a definite programme, the length of time taken at each stage being dependent upon the pony's mental and physical standard. Two old sayings apply very forcibly to the schooling of a young pony :
'More haste, less speed', and 'Make haste slowly'.

The rider

The characteristics of the rider will have a direct bearing on the successful achievement of his objective. He must have an understanding of and a sympathetic attitude towards his pony; a good nerve coupled with boldness and quick thinking will inspire confidence in the pony; firm handling, blended with kindness and sympathy, will induce the pony to rely on his rider and to submit happily and calmly to his requirements.

A sense of anticipation and a power of concentration are important; the rider should have a firm and independent seat so that his indications are accurate, clear, calm and never jumbled; his attitude of position should be sufficiently correct at all times to maintain balance, so that the pony knows where the rider's hand is and is not nervously disturbed by unexpected movements.

The seat is that taught in the Pony Club, with the stirrup leathers shorter for jumping, in order to enable a more forward position to be adopted over the fences. The rider should remain forward until the pony's hind feet are well over the fence. This will entail a slightly shorter rein, if contact and control are to be maintained at all times.

FIGURE 48.   A LOW, STEADY HEAD-CARRIAGE IS DESIRABLE

Training the show jumper

Free forward movement and impulsion must be the first consideration. Balance and suppleness must be developed by suitable exercises. The show jumper must be obedient and responsive to the slightest indication of hand and leg. All this should have been achieved if the pony has been trained on the lines indicated in this book; if not, work must continue and not until he has reached the necessary standard should competitions be attempted.

For show jumping a low head-carriage is desirable. This position encourages and makes easier the rounding of the pony's back, gives freedom of action to the loins and quarters, enables the hocks to engage without effort and so allows the maximum propelling power.   Be sure to teach the pony to lower his head and not put on a martingale in order to achieve this.

Certain movements are of great importance if success in the

ring is to be achieved. Fluid changes of direction, with no loss of rhythm or impulsion, must be made. Lengthening and shortening of the stride must be carried out smoothly without any jerk or loss of balance.

The rein-back should be practised with a view to improving balance and obedience; it should be carried out as previously described. When the backward movement is completed, move smoothly forward first into a walk and, when proficiency is reached, through the paces to a canter.

The use of martingales

Standing martingale. This can be useful on a young pony or one that has been badly trained and throws up his head to evade the bit. It should be fitted at such a length that it does not come into action until the pony's head becomes higher than the point of control ; it should not be fitted to a dropped nose-band. Correctly fitted, it assists control in front of a fence. The disadvantage is that ponies learn to lean against it; this causes stiffness in place of suppleness and develops the wrong muscles of the neck and back and, in extreme cases, a hollow back.

The rider should rather learn how to get a pony's head down without resorting to the martingale, which can only prevent the pony from getting his head up and can never make him keep it down.

Running martingale. If used, this should also be fitted so that it does not come into action unless the head is carried higher than the correct position. It will then help to ensure the proper action of the bit, by controlling the direction of the pull on the reins.

For the correct fitting of the martingale see B.H.S. *Manual of Horsemanship.*

Jumping training

Before attempting to jump show fences, the pony should have been thoroughly trained to jump on the lines described in this book. He will have had loose jumping in the oval lane, and he will have been lunged over a variety of obstacles, including coloured poles and fences of the show ring type. As his training progressed, he will have been ridden over similar practise fences, and also over natural fences out hunting. Not until he will jump all such solid fences cleanly, with zest, freedom, courage and calmness should his training over show fences be undertaken. Faults should have been corrected as they arose as described in this book under 'Correcting jumping faults', and he should now jump anything at which he is presented, in good style.

When dealing with a newly-acquired pony, with whose previous training one is not acquainted, one must first find out the stage which his training has reached and whether he is a natural jumper. Unfortunately many of those to whom jumping comes easily have had their early training neglected; although they jump brilliantly they are often difficult to control. Training, therefore, should consist largely of dressage, and jumping should be on elementary lines until the pony responds correctly to the aids and is properly under control. Time spent on such work will be amply repaid later on.

Every day should start with dressage, the object of which is to get the pony supple and obedient to the aids.

Next should come work at the cavalletti, which will make the pony supple, make him pick up his feet and extend his stride and encourage him to carry his head low and look where he is putting his feet.

The pony should now be ready to be ridden over show fences. These should present no difficulty if his schooling fences have included coloured poles as well as strange looking jumps such as oil drums, straw bales, water troughs, and the like.

The jumps can be scattered about in a paddock and should consist of as great a variety as possible; upright fences and spreads,

FIGURE 49. CAVALLETTI MAKE THE PONY SUPPLE

pole fences a pony can see through and walls which he cannot, white, coloured and natural wood poles, and a ditch with or without water and poles. All should be small.

Commence by using a low pole, followed by parallel bars with one stride in between; for a pony the average will be from 18-20 feet. The pony should approach the pole at a trot, take one canter stride between the fences and jump the parallel bars; these should be kept low; to make the fence larger increase the spread rather than the height. The pole can be moved from in front of one fence to another. When schooling, it is better to circle among the fences and to jump one when the pony is ready, rather than to jump a set course. If the pony jumps correctly another fence may be jumped, but if he rushes or jumps badly, resume the circling. Gradually work up to jumping a small course calmly and in good style. Finish by walking quietly among the fences on a loose rein.

The approach

To ride a course correctly the rider must maintain balance and impulsion, while the pony must be obedient and responsive to the

FIGURE 50.

A LOW BAR FOLLOWED BY A SPREAD FENCE, WITH ONE STRIDE IN BETWEEN

aids. The approach to the fence is the most important part of the round and it begins as soon as the previous fence has been cleared. The rider, therefore, should never look round to see if he has knocked down a fence; all his attention should be concentrated on the fence to come.

To what extent the rider, particularly a young one, should attempt to control the pony's stride, depends upon many factors. Often the pony, especially if he has been well schooled, will meet the fence in his stride; all the rider need do is maintain balance, impulsion, and direction. At other times the rider will realize that the pony must lengthen or shorten his stride. If he is to assist, the rider must have his pony balanced, obedient, and responsive to hand and leg. This is where all the preliminary and dressage training is of such great value.

The ultimate goal, if a speed competition or jump-off against the clock is to be won, is to attain precision at speed – and this entails a very high degree of control, both on the approach and during the whole round.

When cornering at a canter, the pony should lead with the inside leg. Provided he is balanced and has been well trained, he will change of his own accord when making a sharp turn. If he becomes disunited, a slight increase of pace will rectify matters; if, on a wide turn, he does not change, no great harm will be done for he should be accustomed to jumping off either leg. If the rider is continually asking the pony to change, he is liable to unsettle him.

Combination fences: doubles and trebles

As a test of a pony's jumping ability and training, combination fences are included in all courses. The distance between fences varies according to the type of fence, upright or spread. These combination fences test, amongst other things, the ability of the pony to lengthen his stride and to 'stand back', and also to shorten his stride and 'arch' over an upright fence. Every rider should know the distances which suit his own mount so that, having walked the course and paced the distances between combination fences, he will realize the speed at which he must approach, and the number of strides to be taken between the different jumps.

When approaching combination fences the rider should 'aim' at the centre of the last one; it is surprising how often neglect of this principle involves a 'run-out'.

Conclusion

To sum up: what is required is a free, bold pony, well balanced, supple and responsive to the rider's aids. This is achieved by orthodox training on the flat – dressage – and over small fences of great variety.

The rider must have a firm and independent seat, maintaining contact with hand and leg; his position must be balanced, his aids accurate and clear.

Above all, good jumping requires a combination of pony and rider based on true understanding and sound basic training in which both have shared.

FIGURE 51.
A BOLD, OBEDIENT PONY, RESPONSIVE TO THE RIDER'S AIDS

APPENDIX C

PRODUCING A SHOW PONY

Before we start let us consider for a moment the judges before whom we are going to show our ponies.

It is not easy to be a judge, but it is the job of a good competitor to try to 'sell' his productions to the judge, and nothing that art or skill can do should be left undone to attain this end. If, however, you show under a judge who does not like your pony, in spite of the fact that all other judges to date have put it on top, take your beating in a sportsmanlike manner, and do not run whimpering the press correspondent.

To produce a show pony really well requires careful attention to detail. So often one sees good ponies badly produced; and equally, a less than top pony can get the highest honours if well produced and ridden.

Be sure that you keep to the rules – that your pony is not over height, or ridden by someone over age, and that, if entered as a novice, it is really so.

First make sure that you really have a pony which is up to the standard you aspire to. Some people have a wonderful eye for animals in the rough, but they are few, so get a very knowledge-able person to help you to make a good selection to start with. This is so important and will save much heartbreak later.

Have the pony carefully examined for age and for soundness. You are entitled to insist on any veterinary inspection, but if you have chosen the veterinary surgeon and things subsequently go wrong, you have no claim against the vendor.

Having bought the pony, look after him properly. Dose him for worms, and get his digestion right before doing anything more. You can do little until he is looking and feeling well.

The ideal time to buy a pony for showing the following season, is in the autumn. Feed him very well all the winter. There are many different schools of thought on the type of feed, but he will want bulky feeds and plenty of linseed oil during the winter. Towards the spring, begin to get the pony fit by slow exercise, until the fat has become muscle. Then, and only then, ask him to work. Do not make the common mistake of over-schooling – endless figures of eight, cantering, and circles. Of course the pony must be taught to do these things as well as to stand well, and to run out well in hand. But he wants plenty of quiet hacking in between. Increasing and decreasing pace on a straight line is often more valuable than too much training on a circle, after you have established a good rhythm at the lungeing stage. It is not easy to get ponies well schooled and there are, sadly, too many people who spoil good material for lack of knowledge.

It is often much better to start breaking your own pony yourself. This is done on the lunge, as described on pages 11 to 15.

Trimming for the show must be well done; no hairs on jaws, heels, or ears; a well pulled mane, not too thick, and a well pulled tail. Do not brush or comb your show pony's tail; clean the top of the tail with a body brush and wash the ends. During the day the

FIGURE 52.   THE SHOW PONY

tail must be well bandaged, but do not leave the bandages on all night. White hooves must be scrubbed and socks washed and whitened.

Plaits should be tiny and neat, and should help whatever line the neck requires. A poor neck can thus be given an extra two inches by clever plaiting.

Rugging and bandaging are both helpful and necessary to get the top-gloss effect, but good strapping and first class condition are the most important features.

After this comes the problem of putting the pony in the ring in the right frame of mind, and going just right for his rider's capabilities. Nothing but careful exercise and feeding, in relation to the pony's temperament, will ensure this. Many a time it is necessary to ride from 4 a.m. to 6 a.m. to ensure this. There is really no short cut if you wish to succeed and you can afford to leave no stone unturned.

APPENDIX D

TRAINING A PONY FOR POLO

The training of a reasonable riding pony up to a standard to make it an enjoyable mount for paddock polo, or polo up to medium class, is not a formidable task, probably far less so than most people, who have not tried it, imagine. Of course the difficulties encountered and the time required will vary according to the individual pony and the standard aimed at.

The aim

What is required is an animal that will answer the leg and the reins, used in one hand, quickly and easily; in other words, one that will go and stop, change direction either way, and stop, turn about and go again; also one that will not mind the stick used on either side of him and will be true on the ball.

Equipment

(1) The first requirement is a reasonable flat and smooth piece of ground on which a rectangular manege of approximately 40 yards by 20 yards can be marked out. The exact size and shape are of no importance. It can be marked out by sticks, stones or anything else convenient, or at times even just kept in the mind's eye, if it is desired to do a little schooling whilst hacking about the fields.

(2) A polo stick, the length of which should approximately conform to the height of the pony. 50 in. or 51 in. is a normal length for a 15 h.h. pony. 46 in. to 48 in. would probably be about right for a 14 h.h. pony, and other lengths in proportion.

(3) A few polo balls; perhaps one large soft one and four or five ordinary ones.

(4) Boots or bandages for the pony's legs.

(5) A reasonable sized field of smooth, short grass if possible, on which to knock the ball about.

Training

Start off in the manege doing the simple exercises that were taught in the early stages of the training of the pony:

Simple turns and circles;
Inclines across the manege, changing the rein;
Short figures of eight;
Turns across the manege, changing the rein;
Circles in the corners.

Do these first at the trot, with the reins in both hands. When the pony is going well, with the reins in both hands continue the same exercise with the reins in the left hand, using the neck rein, i.e. carrying the rein hand slightly over to the left or right according to which way the pony is required to turn, so that the outside rein bears on the pony's neck, acting as an additional aid in asking him to change direction.

It is essential that the pony should do these exercises quietly and on a loose rein. If he will not go on a loose rein to begin with, patience and perseverance must be exercised until he will. A neck strap of some sort may be found helpful in restraining him, rather than using the reins; the voice can also be of assistance.

When the pony is going well at these exercises at the trot, introduce the halt among them. The object is to get the pony's hocks right underneath him, taking nearly all the weight, with practically no weight on the forehand. The voice may well be used as an additional aid in halting. A fairly staccato 'halt', or probably better 'hup', at the same time as the other aids are applied is undoubtedly a help, and the pony very soon learns what is required when he hears it.

When the pony has come to a halt, after a momentary pause ask him to rein-back a few paces.

When satisfied with the rein-back up to four distinct paces, ease the hands, use a strong leg aid, and the pony should move forward again almost at a bound from the hocks, as from a spring. This halt, rein-back and forward again exercise can be introduced anywhere amongst the other exercises, though best – to begin with at any rate – only when moving on a straight line along the side or the end of the manege, or when turning across the manege. When this is going well, the next movement to introduce is the turnabout.

To do this, halt and rein-back, but at the end of the rein-back, before moving forward again, make the pony turn about on his hocks either to the right or the left. The aids are: continue strong pressure with both legs to keep the pony's hocks well under him, then carry the reins over to the right or left and use the outside leg strongly, and the pony should pivot round on his hind legs with no weight on his forehand at all. As soon as he is round, use the same aids as before to make him move forward, now going in the opposite direction to that in which he was going before.

The importance of the rider using a strong and correct aid to the halt, so as to bring the pony's hocks well under him, cannot be too strongly emphasized. It is absolutely essential for the hocks to come right underneath the pony and to take nearly all the weight, so that practically no weight is left on the forehand. Merely to pull on the reins so that the pony halts with his hocks sprawled out behind him and all the weight on his forehand is as useless for making a polo pony as at any other time.

So far the pony has not been asked to go faster than a trot and nothing at all rough or violent has been done, even over the halt, rein-back and move forward again. The object has been to get him going quietly and kindly on a loose rein, obeying the leg and the neck rein, to get his hocks under him, and his forehand light when halting and moving forward again, and to get him supple.

As soon as he is going quietly and kindly in these exercises at a trot, some gentle cantering can be begun. But it is most important to avoid hotting him up. He must continue to go quietly and on a loose rein. It now becomes necessary to change legs whenever direction is changed. At the canter or gallop a pony must be leading with his inside leg when going on a circle, or he may well cross his legs and fall.

It is most strongly recommended that, until a very advanced stage has been reached by both rider and pony, no attempt should be, made while schooling in the manege, to do the flying change at the canter. When a change of direction is made, bring the pony back to a trot and make him strike off on the other leg. The fewer trotting paces there are, the better. Gradually improve this until he just comes to a trot for one or two paces and strikes off again with the other leg leading. But he must always be made to strike off correctly, and at all costs the rider must avoid the common error of leaning down to see if he is right.

The other exercises necessary in the training of a polo pony are those to teach the pony to go sideways away from the leg. This is an important part of the training of a good pony (See pages 76-78).

Some ponies will go away from the leg quite easily, others may be very stubborn and difficult to teach and much patience may be necessary. With difficult ones it is often best to dismount and, standing beside them, make them go away from the hand or pressure of a stick. They will generally do this quite easily. After doing this several times, mount and try again. An excellent occasion to teach a pony to go away from the leg is while walking along a road. A difficult pony can quite often be made to do a gentle half pass backwards and forwards across a road without realizing that it is being asked to do anything special. For a polo pony it is not really necessary to demand the correct bend and flexion of the head and neck when doing these lateral movements, as it is for dressage, though lessons in obedience and muscling exercises are undoubtedly better if the pony is made to bend correctly. But to go quickly and actively sideways when the leg is applied is the important thing.

During all the time this training has been going on, training in stick and ball can also be carried on simultaneously. The first thing is to get the pony accustomed to the stick and fearless of it, without a ball. First of all let the pony see the stick and sniff at it before attempting to mount him with it. It is quite a good thing to have a few hanging round his stable and by his haynet. When mounting a pony with a polo stick, hold the stick in the left hand round the binding at the small end of the stick with the hand up against the head of the stick, and the handle down towards the ground. Then when properly mounted, quietly take the stick in the right hand, holding the handle right up at the end of the stick, except when hitting the ball or swinging the stick for a definite purpose. When riding a pony with a stick or when actually playing polo, always carry the stick 'at the slope', – the handle leaning lightly against the right shoulder with the head up in the air. Nothing is more inclined to make a pony shy off and to stop him galloping, than a rider who carries his stick pointing round about his head. The only other way to carry a stick when mounted, and when not actually using it, is upside down with the hand close up by the head of the stick, and the stick running slightly behind the leg like a whip, and pointing to the ground.

When mounted on a pony for the first-time with a stick, get him going well and very quietly before very gently starting to swing the stick, first on the offside and then on the nearside. Few ponies will give much trouble with this and, with those that do, a little patience will generally affect a cure. The greatest care must of course be taken not to hit the pony with the stick, particularly on the head or the legs.

When the pony is going quite quietly and happily with the stick, and taking no notice of it when swung on either side of him, a ball may be introduced. Whenever attempting to knock a ball about, the pony should have boots or bandages on. Boots are undoubtedly better than bandages as, if of good design, they will give some protection to the fetlock joints and the pasterns which are the most vulnerable and important parts. Bandages, which must not of course be put over the joints, give no protection to these.

Ponies often make more fuss about the ball than they do over the stick, but this is probably more often due to naughtiness than fear. They will very soon get over any fear of the ball, particularly

FIGURE 53. ON THE BALL

if some are left in and around their stables or fields. Great care must always be taken, particularly in the early stages, to avoid hitting them on the legs with the ball. Start knocking the ball about at the walk and if things go well, gradually work up to a trot and a canter. Equally, start with the easier shots and only gradually work up to the more difficult nearside shots, etc. When knocking about, have several balls lying about if possible and when hitting, always try to aim at something, one of the other balls will do as an aiming mark. Accuracy is far more valuable than great length. If you miss the ball do not pull up immediately and have another go, ride on to another ball if there is one, or make the pony go straight on for a certain distance before pulling up or turning round.

Equally, when hitting a backhander, do not turn the pony about immediately the ball has been hit, or he will very soon start anticipating and turning almost before the shot is made, which makes it much more difficult. Always make him go on in the same straight line a few more paces after the shot has been made, before turning him about.

When making any shot with the stick, it is most important not to job the pony in the mouth. To avoid any possibility of this it is quite a good habit to let the left hand go forward a little and ease the reins as the stick is swung.

Finally, unless a reasonably flat, smooth field can be found, with fairly short grass, it is probably better not to attempt knocking a ball about. Trying to knock about on rough ground with long tussocky grass, when the ball will neither travel any distance nor go straight, and continually has to be dug out of the grass, almost certainly does more harm than good both to the rider and to the pony, and to the tempers of both.

APPENDIX E

POINT-TO-POINTS

There are a number of Pony Club associates who have well-bred, well-schooled animals and who would like to 'have a go' in the point-to-points. It is to help those who perhaps have no experienced person to turn to, that these notes have been written.

Planning ahead

The point-to-point season opens in mid-February and comes to an end in mid-May. The horse must be ready to go into training at the beginning of January. To be ready in time entails thinking well ahead, probably at the end of the previous season – earlier if one has to buy a horse.

For those new to the business it is wise to get a copy of the *Regulations for Point-to-Point Steeplechases*, published by Messrs.

Weatherby, 15 Cavendish Square, London, w.1. From these much can be learnt about qualifying a horse, which horses and riders are eligible, particulars of adjacent hunt and other races, and other information which, if assimilated, will save disappointment later on.

If you do not own a suitable horse and want to buy one, it is as well to realize the high standard of point-to-point races which, in general, require a good thoroughbred horse to win them. Whether buying a horse privately or at one of the bloodstock sales, it is essential to have the advice of an experienced person and to have the horse examined by a veterinary surgeon.

Early training

No horse may run at under five years of age, but six is a better age at which to start. If his training has followed the lines suggested in this book he will be ready to run in point-to-points at the end of his five-year-old season. In the case of a new purchase, steps must be taken to discover how fit he is, how much he knows, and to improve his training where necessary. His mouth and jumping are two obvious matters which must be attended to.

For the horse which has been trained by the owner on sound lines and is being hunted as a five-year-old, no special training will be required during the season, except as described under 'Hunting'.

Hunting and qualifying

The owner must decide, if there is any choice, with which hunt the horse is to be qualified, as this will affect the adjacent hunts' races in which he can run. No horse may receive more than two certificates and only one may be used for adjacent hunts' races. To receive a certificate, a horse must be 'regularly and fairly hunted'; this generally means eight to ten days. It is as well to aim at qualifying the horse by the new year, to allow for lameness or bad weather; only days' hunting after the opening meet count.

Condition is a matter of months and years rather than weeks; one may take the previous spring as a starting point and at this time the horse should have his teeth attended to and be treated for worms, if necessary, before being put out to grass; here will be laid the foundation on which his condition will be built. It may be decided to keep the horse up and in light work during the summer, but if the horse is to go out he must have good grass, clean water, shade and shelter, and be visited regularly. If he is not doing well his field must be changed or he can be brought in – perhaps only by day if the flies are bad.

As the horse must be really fit during the hunting season, he must be brought in from grass in good time, preferably about the end of July, and given regular work from the beginning of August. He must be really big, fit and well by the end of October, in time for the opening meet. During the season he must be made as hard as nails and muscular, but he should not have long days or become jaded or weary. When he goes into training in January he must still be big, fit and well, and must not be allowed to run up light to become stiff or leg weary. Most horses enjoy hunting and it improves their jumping and makes them clever and careful, but they must not be over-hunted. It is hard enough to keep a horse fresh when he is in training; he must not start stale.

Training

The average horse, which has been regularly hunted, needs about a month in training before his first race. The object of this training is to produce him at the top of his form, or slightly below for the first race.

And here it must be emphasized that every animal, like every human being, is different, and that the great art of training lies in the study of the individual, his likes and dislikes, his good points and weaknesses, and arranging his feeding, exercise and races accordingly.

Stable management is the foundation of condition and must be first class. He will need plenty of good food and to be fed at least three times a day, the biggest feed being in the evening and the smallest in the morning. The amount of oats will increase as training progresses; they should be lightly crushed, and a bran mash should be given once or twice a week. He will also receive appetizers such as carrots, apple, beans, raw eggs, stout, molasses, or green food. Hay must be of the best, two years old, and not dusty; it should be shaken to get the dust out of it. A horse in training will not need so much hay as when hunting. Great attention should be paid to grooming and wisping, which is an excellent massage and tones up the muscles. The best part of half an hour at midday and evening stables should be given to this; wisping mostly in the evening.

Whether he is looking after the horse himself or not, the owner should go carefully round the horse every evening at stables, especially, feeling the legs and examining the feet.

Exercise and work

First one must get the horse really well in himself, in good health, muscled up and on his toes. Then he must be taught to jump fast. Finally his wind must be got straight.

The training programme will be considered week by week, assuming that a month is available before the first race.

First two weeks. Probably the commonest mistake is to start with too much fast work. It is better to begin with easy work. The horse should be made to walk out and not to idle along; the trot should be steady but active, with the horse on the bit. Exercise is of little use if the horse does not use himself properly and move with a long stride. Fast trotting is always bad, especially on hard roads; a gentle hill on downs, moors or old turf is best. About an hour or an hour-and-a-half of this work would be sufficient at first.

Fast work will not start for at least a week and then it will consist of half-speed gallops of six furlongs to a mile. During the second week, probably three days will be spent on slow work on the turf, with faster work on alternate days. The distance will be increased to one and a half or even two miles, but still at half-speed. The corn ration can be correspondingly increased to 16–18 lb., provided the horse will eat it, but it may be found that as he gets really fit he will not eat quite as much.

By the *third week* the horse should be getting straight in all but his wind, and he should work in company, increasing to three-parts speed and going well on the bit.

About this time, schooling over fences should begin. Assuming him to be a good jumper in the hunting field, he must learn to jump more quickly and to stand back and reach for his fences. Schooling should be in company and start at a strong canter, probably over bushed hurdles and then over fences, one of which should be an open ditch. Schools will normally take place before fast work and will consist of jumping about three fences once or twice.

The fast work will be on alternate days, exercise on the other three consisting of walking and trotting, preferably on the soft and uphill, changing the route daily.

All the time it is important to watch the horse carefully. Is he 'eating up'? Is he getting appetizers and enjoying his food? Is he eating quietly and steadily?

At work, is he going well and freely? Is he on the bit at the end of a gallop? Is his breathing free and clear, or is he labouring? Watch his flanks.

The object during the *fourth week* is to get the horse's wind clear. Be careful with the hay – he must not have too much and it must not be dusty.

The work must be faster and the distances shorter and, with most horses, should be done in company. Begin with a five- or six-furlong canter, followed by a sharp six furlongs or a mile, depending on the horse.

On one or two days, according to how he is jumping, there will be another school over the fences, again in company. The horse should be ridden strongly into his fences and made to stand well away and reach for them, without any dwelling, getting smoothly away on landing.

The horse must be watched carefully in these final stages; above all he must not be over-trained. His first race will bring him on a lot, but if he is at all over-trained he will soon begin to go stale.

The day before the race he may have a pipe-opener of four or five furlongs. What he does on the morning of the race depends on the horse, the time he has to spend in the box, the hour at which he leaves home, the time of the race and the facilities for giving him a pipe-opener on the way to the start. He will need to go a couple of furlongs at home or on the course.

He should have very little hay the night before his race and no fresh straw; his ration may be made up with a few more oats.

Only· experience and watching and studying the horse very carefully can bring him under starter's orders trained to the minute.

The rider

A few remarks addressed to the rider who has not ridden in a race before may not be out of place.

The horse should be ridden in a snaffle, preferably of the 'egg-butt' type, without a martingale. 'Rings' or an Irish martingale are a useful addition. The rider must get a light saddle or at any rate, if weight is no problem, one which is cut well forward and which will allow him to shorten his stirrups and adopt a proper position when galloping and jumping.

In the Pony Club film 'Jumping' there are excellent photographs of a leading professional and a leading amateur riding over fences and hurdles. Much can be learned from this film which shows the proper way to ride and some amusing mistakes.

Whether or not this film is available, watch the professionals riding over fences, and study photographs. Note how the expert sits still, leaning well forward to lessen wind resistance, allowing his horse to gallop under him, with his seat just clear of·the saddle. How he drops his seat into the saddle and drives his horse into the fence, making him take-off well away. The expert can ride with a long rein and bent elbow which enables him to give the horse

FIGURE 54.   WINNING THE LADIES' RACE

plenty of rein over the fence. If the horse hits the fence and blunders, or if the rider gets 'left behind' by a big stand-off, he will allow the reins to slip through his fingers so that his position remains secure even if the horse's head is nearly on the ground. Short reins held by a firm, unyielding grip can easily result in the jockey being quickly pulled over the horse's head, in the case of a mistake. The beginner should learn the 'drill' of shortening his reins after slipping them, and getting up on his knees again quickly as his horse gets away from a fence. He must remember to keep hold of his horse's head all the time and especially in a finish. He should be chary of using a whip until he has learned how, or he will find that he loses more races with it than without it.

INDEX